ATWOOD'S *THE H*

Continuum Reader's Guides

Continuum Reader's Guides are clear, concise and accessible introductions to classic literary texts. Each book explores the themes, context, criticism and influence of key works, providing a practical introduction to close reading and guiding the reader towards a thorough understanding of the text. Ideal for undergraduate students, the guides provide an essential resource for anyone who needs to get to grips with a literary text.

Achebe's *Things Fall Apart* – Ode Ogede
Austen's *Emma* – Gregg A. Hecimovich
Bronte's *Wuthering Heights* – Ian Brinton
Bram Stoker's *Dracula* William Hughes
Chaucer's *The Canterbury Tales* – Gail Ashton
Conrad's *Heart of Darkness* – Allan Simmons
Dickens's *Great Expectations* – Ian Brinton
Eliot's *Middlemarch* – Josie Billington
Fitzgerald's *The Great Gatsby* – Nicolas Tredell
Fowles's *The French Lieutenant's Woman* – William Stephenson
James's *The Turn of the Screw* – Leonard Orr
Joyce's *Ulysses* – Sean Sheehan
Salinger's *The Catcher in the Rye* – Sarah Graham
William Blake's *Poetry* – Jonathan Roberts
Woolf's *To the Lighthouse* – Janet Winston

ATWOOD'S
THE HANDMAID'S TALE

A READER'S GUIDE

GINA WISKER

continuum

Continuum International Publishing Group
The Tower Building   80 Maiden Lane
11 York Road   Suite 704
London SE1 7NX   New York, NY 10038

www.continuumbooks.com

British Library Cataloguing-in-Publication Data
A catalogue record for this book is available from the British
Library.

ISBN: 978-0-8264-6362-3 (hardback)
        978-0-8264-2601-7 (paperback)

Library of Congress Cataloging-in-Publication Data
A catalog record for this book is available from the Library of
Congress.

Typeset by Newgen Imaging Systems Pvt Ltd, Chennai, India
Printed and bound in Great Britain by MPG Books Group Ltd

To

All the Women's Studies and English Literature students who
have worked with me and contributed such good ideas to
studying this and other work by Margaret Atwood – at
Anglia Ruskin University, the University of Brighton
and Madingley Hall, Cambridge University
And to Alistair, Liam and Kitt

CONTENTS

ACKNOWLEDGEMENTS

The Handmaid's Tale has always been my favourite novel by Margaret Atwood, in the main because of the way in which it has inspired, provoked and interested so many literature and women's studies students undergraduate and postgraduate in continuing education at Anglia Ruskin University, and the universities of Brighton and Cambridge. I should like to thank all my students who have discussed the book and its implications with me, over the years. I should like to thank Tracy Kellock for her unstinting professional help supporting the development of this book from start to finish, Jennifer Toewes and Philip Oldfield of the Thomas Fisher rare book library, University of Toronto for making Atwood's papers and the critical works available to me and my Dean Paul Griffiths and Pro-Vice Chancellor Stuart Laing of the University of Brighton for letting me fly over there to access the work. Finally thanks to Margaret Atwood's publishers.

QUOTATIONS AND ABBREVIATIONS

All references to Atwood's *The Handmaid's Tale* are to the 1987 edition, London: Virago.

The following abbreviation has been used:

HT   *The Handmaid's Tale*

CHAPTER 1

CONTEXT

Margaret Atwood is an internationally renowned, highly versatile writer whose work, comprising poetry, novels, short stories, literary criticism and essays has been translated into more than 20 languages and published in over 25 countries. Recognized as a feminist author, and the greatest living Canadian writer, engaged with issues of gendered and national identity, she also problematizes both of these labels and trends in her work. She is, above all, a creative explorer of what it means to be human and how this can be expressed through the strategies and genres of fiction, language and narrative.

She was born on 18 November 1939, in Ottawa, Ontario, the second of three children. Until she was 12 she spent most of her summers in the wilds of the northern bush country of Quebec and Ontario with her family. Dividing time between the bush and the town helped develop a sense of dual identity and allegiance which has informed both the imagery and ideas in her work. In 1946 her family moved to Toronto, where she attended high school (1952–1957). Between 1957 and 1961 she studied Honours English (with the critic Northrop Frye and Jay Macpherson) at Victoria College, the University of Toronto, graduating in 1961.

Atwood was initially known for her poetry, which deals with respect for the possibilities of language underpinning her ability to express forms of perception and to demystify the stereotypes, the personal, national or gendered myths and representations by which we conceive and manage our lives.

Margaret Atwood's first collection of poetry was a privately printed, self-published chapbook, *Double Persephone*, which won the E. J. Pratt medal in 1961. She won a Woodrow Wilson Fellowship which enabled her to become a graduate student at Radcliffe College, Harvard University, Massachusetts. In 1962 she gained her MA and began to read for a PhD at Harvard on 'The English Metaphysical Romance'. Deciding that academic life (or at least academic research) was not for her, after all, she interrupted her studies to work for a market research company in Toronto and to teach English at the University of British Columbia in Vancouver (1964 1965). Here she wrote the first draft of *The Edible Woman* which was published in 1969. In 1966 she published *The Circle Game*, which received the Governor General's Award for Poetry. *The Animals in that Country* appeared in 1968; with *The Journals of Susanna Moodie* and *Procedures for Underground* (both 1970), and *Power Politics* (1971), Atwood established herself as an important poet and then as an equally important novelist. The publication in 1972 of both *Surfacing* and *Survival: A Thematic Guide to Canadian Literature* consolidated her significance as a novelist and a cultural critic.

Margaret Atwood has lived primarily in Canada, with spells in the US, and Europe. She has won the Governor General's Award twice (1966 and 1986); the Welsh Arts Council International Writer's Prize (1982); the Los Angeles Times Prize for Fiction (1986), and has been several times shortlisted for the Booker Prize, which she won with *The Blind Assassin* in 2000. She is politically and socially involved through PEN and Amnesty International and continues to be active against social injustice. Atwood's work is read throughout the world and both *Surfacing* and *The Handmaid's Tale* have been made into films.

GENRE FICTIONS

Her interventions into literary and popular fictional genres, such as Gothic romance, spy thriller, science fiction, feminist fable, comedy and crime fiction have enabled the re-scrutinizing of those genres. Jeremy Brooks, (*The Sunday Times,* 27 May 1973) praises her perception and imaginative expression, noting 'the balance between the narrator's interior vision and sharp observation of the real world'. Her writing has had a significant influence on contemporary writing by women, and has brought the re-writing of genre fiction to the fore as a form of cultural critique in postmodernist and other contemporary writing. Many of her works rewrite romantic fictions, while *The Handmaid's Tale* rewrites science fiction and utopian fiction forms.

CONTEMPORARY CONCERNS

Comparing the context of then, the 1980s, and now, is very important for a contemporary reader. We need to understand what the issues, trends and concerns were in the 1980s which produced this novel and how Atwood looked forward through her dystopian fiction, to a world where the worst that could happen has happened, and where some of the hopes, such as for a world where women were really important, had actually not led to quite the outcome that was hoped for. We inevitably look at the concerns of the novel in context of the 1980s and in our own context and will find some of it surprisingly fresh and frightening as it takes current trends one step further to their possible resolutions, while some other events and trends which Atwood was concerned about have perhaps been resolved, in the years between 1987 and now. We need to be reading with two contexts at least in mind.

Atwood's work engages with modernist and postmodernist philosophical concerns, with the nature of reality, history and identity. She has tackled a whole range of conventions, social, personal and political issues, from sisterhood to reproductive technologies, eating disorders to identity theft, and in her dystopian novels, of which *The Handmaid's Tale* is one and the recent *Oryx and Crake*, the other, she looks at the dire consequences of contemporary behaviours and mistakes, in the latter novel focusing on the end of the world as we know it, a logical next step on from current trends in anti-emotional, anti-artistic, scientific rationalism and dehumanization.

The Handmaid's Tale was published in 1985, in a period in which second wave feminism flourished, and much of her concerns here are with issues of women's lives, freedoms, procreation and rights over their own bodies. It was also a period of the rise of fundamentalist religious regimes, especially in Iran, which Atwood visited just prior to writing the novel. Since the novel's publication, second wave feminism has flowered and been replaced by post-feminism and third wave feminism, what this means in effect is that the idealistic values and visions often (or seems with hindsight) extreme visions of equality and sisterhood have been undermined and questioned, and women have also during the intervening years gained a great deal of economic equality; in the US Hillary Clinton ran for president and might have won as the first woman president if she had not been overtaken by the first black president Barack Obama. In the UK in the 1980s we had Margaret Thatcher the first woman prime minister. While there is still economic inequality and the glass ceiling in terms of job opportunities where women somehow find they cannot reach the top of organizations, there is nonetheless a more equal society at least in the UK, US and Australasia. However, in Iran and Iraq and other parts of the world where religious fundamentalism has taken hold, there is often extreme inequality, ironically and worryingly many of Atwood's predictions about excluding women from education, (no woman is allowed to read or write in *The Handmaid's Tale*) have been fulfilled in areas under the control of the Taliban.

Her interest in the ways in which we construct versions of our lives, tell stories, reconstruct and reflect was one common in that period and it has become even more so in the intervening years. John Barth and Thomas Pynchon in the US, for example, and Doris Lessing with *The Golden Notebook*, each focused on the ways in which we construct versions of stories in order to make sense of the world and our place in it. They looked also at how these versions substitute for reality we cannot otherwise grasp, because we all live through making sense of the world and events in it and this sense making is the fundamental element of storytelling. Such a belief is based on the philosophical influence of writers such as the phenomenologists Edmund Husserl, Maurice Merleau-Ponty and Jean-Paul Sartre who also, in different ways, identified how the being in the world, the person, makes sense (or not) through using language, through establishing themselves in relation to other living things and in context. The world can be seen as a construction and our role within it as a performance. This can lead to a sense of anxiety and dismay in contrast to the certainties of beliefs where we are sure we know the real world and share it with others. However, versions of the realisation of the performance of our lives and the constructedness of ways we make sense of and label the world have passed into everyday language and exchange since the 1970s when they were popular in US and UK literature. Politically we have also seen the rise of regimes which resemble those of *The Handmaid's Tale*, while Iran was repressive in the 1980s, Iraq has been seen to be more repressive in the twenty-first century and Pakistan as a nuclear threat. Fears about technology and reproduction, lack of fertility due to pollution and misuse of the earth's resources have all grown in the years between so that the issues of sustainable development, of the planet's sustainability and the need to regulate toxins in the water, pollutants in the air and in our food have all become the harsh reality of our world rather than just a bleak fictional vision in Atwood's novel. So in this sense she was ahead of her time as one would expect from a dystopian fiction – where the aim is to identify the problems of the day (she was talking of the 1980s at that time), and imagine them forwards into worst case scenarios – reproductive technologies, fundamentalist religious regimes, and a polluted world of wars between religious factions, a life without the modern comforts we take for granted, with a cruel regime which punishes any kind of difference. The sons of Ham (African American) and Jews are persecuted, and gay men and lesbians killed, as are doctors and abortionists whose views about birth control and regulation go against the regime's emphasis on procreation in the midst of sterility.

CANADIAN WRITING

Atwood is perceived as probably the leading living Canadian writer. Since the 1970s she has been a critical pioneer bringing the work of other Canadian writers to an international readership and the lives, histories and values of other Canadians into a more public view with her own fictions, criticism and poetry.

Her work began to receive international critical attention in 1972, with the publication of her novel *Surfacing* and her influential critical analysis of Canada's literary tradition up until that time, *Survival: A Thematic Guide to Canadian Literature*. Canadian literature, or 'Can lit', as an established identified location for study, has only really emerged since around 1980.

Much of Margaret Atwood's work concentrates on exploring and rewriting representations of Canada and what it means to be Canadian. It investigates, rewrites and updates the pioneering versions of history, setting these against contemporary tales of Canadians. She rewrites and critiques cultural and traditional myths frequently using these to explore and represent histories and stories of women and of the people of Toronto. This city features as a location in many of her works including *The Blind Assassin* and *Cat's Eye*. However, the themes and concerns of her novels, as of *The Handmaid's Tale* are also generalizable to many other locations and contexts, to other societies and places and so they speak to us as readers whether we are located in the US, Canada, UK, or Australasia, Europe, the Caribbean. The Canadian context is noticeable in *The Handmaid's Tale* as Canada features as a place for relative equality and security while the US has been polluted, has undergone terrible wars and reverted to a version of religious fundamentalism which operates a class system based on fertility or lack of it, and patriarchal power.

Considering Atwood as a Canadian writer means recognizing the relationship between the US and Canada where the US is often seen as a brasher more powerful neighbour and Canada as more liberal and tolerant, less warlike. Atwood's work and its popularity has opened up the study of other Canadian writers worldwide and a few of the other important Canadian writers deserve some consideration. The work of other Canadian writers such as Margaret Laurence, Alice Munro, Carol Shields, Michael Ondaatje and First Nations writers in order to contextualize Atwood's work and further her own engagement with Canadian literature and our understanding of its concerns and forms.

CULTURAL CONTEXTS AND ISSUES

The intellectual and cultural context in which her work is being read and has been read is increasingly one which focuses on and problematizes divisions of power in relation to gender, ethnicity and religion. The treatment of these issues in Atwood's text is so much more relevant in the early twenty-first century in the context of religious fundamentalism and erosion of the hitherto taken for granted equal rights of women in many contexts.

Much contemporary women's writing engages with gender and politics, cultural difference and issues of reproductive rights while much contemporary postmodernist writing problematizes the trustworthiness and fixed nature of history and other constructions of 'reality'. These are all concerns explored in the range of her work.

CHAPTER 2

OVERVIEW OF THEMES

This chapter looks at a range of key themes which run throughout the novel. You might find your own themes or other examples of these themes in action. Critical issues include the focus of feminism on constructions and representations of gender, postmodernist comments on the fallibility of recorded history, genre fictions and dystopias, as well as feminist fiction, historical tales and the intersections with mysteries and autobiographies.

Themes which emerge are:

a. Women and feminism: Representation of women's roles, constraints, gender, sexuality and power, the management and control of reproductive rights, feminist themes, issues and reading practices, concerns with women's lives, gender roles and performativity. Reproductive technologies and controls over women's bodies.

b. Language, style and form. Narrative practices, autobio graphy and versions of history, who to trust and how language manipulates experiences and records. Language play. The power of language and silence.

c. Dystopias and genre fictions – their focus and characteristics, dystopia and projections of the faults and potential problems of the present into this novel. More generally considering Atwood's use of and interventions in genres and to what effects. Genre fictions and their engagement with popular cultural and imaginative worlds.

d. Power, control and religious fundamentalism.

In so doing this chapter introduces and explores key questions such as –

- How does the novel deal with the contradictions in the treatment and representation of women?
- How can feminist readings deal with this?

- How can narratives and stories ever represent history and experience?
- How do we construct personae through storytelling and autobiography?
- Where is the truth about Offred and events?
- How can scholarship (the professor at the end) ever represent history and truth?
- How does a dystopian fiction work to enable an exploration and warning about possible futures?

The Handmaid's Tale can be read in several ways, each related to themes which run throughout Atwood's work. As a novel which appeared to acclaim from feminist critics, it provides an exploration of questions about the control of women's bodies, the intrusion of reproductive technologies and the ways in which language operates as power to repress self, control sexuality and limit freedoms. It is also a novel which questions histories and the ways in which we construct them, as in the later *Alias Grace*, for we are dependant for the story on Offred, Handmaid and holocaust survivor, on her own journal rescued and placed in an archive in a distant future, where her words transcribed from a tape recording are viewed by yet another male controlling authority figure, the professor, who treats her as part of an archive, as undependable and only marginally interesting. Throughout the novel we focus on a mix of fantastic or realistic futures, which invites us to consider the individual experiences of a very well realized character, Offred; ways of making or expressing this history and the construction of historical versions and versions of the real; worrying current trends which could lead to future scenarios such as those explored in *The Handmaid's Tale,* and perhaps behaviours which might avoid the worst elements of The Republic of Gilead, in which the novel is set.

We also consider how language and narrative formats construct and confirm or question realities and interpretations by using a mixture of the modes of myth and autobiography, the formats and characteristics of official records, including academic texts. All of these are used in *The Handmaid's Tale* to record Offred's life, to represent the history of her mother's and her generation, or to indicate the ways in which histories received and reconstructed in future times are based on the undependable flotsam, jetsam and official records of the lives of the past, and so the way they are interpreted as history can vary enormously.

Links between power, sexuality and language are very important in the novel which is influenced by and can be read using theories developed by Michel Foucault (1978) who identifies ways in which power, through language, controls sexuality, identity and sexual freedoms. He also writes about surveillance, which is widely used to control people's behaviour in Gilead. Atwood expresses ways in which language reveals or hides, how irony and ambiguous language can enable some freedoms of thought.

In order to explore these themes, each is introduced and discussed here in an introductory, overall fashion, although you will find that they emerge and are treated in depth as they develop in Chapter 3 of this book. That chapter takes you carefully through each of the sections and the chapters and explores, explains and raises questions using discussion and some close detailed reading. In this respect, you might like to look at the first few opening pages of the novel, which lead the reader into all the key themes, issues, problems, and concerns about language and representation of events, as well as introducing the protagonist, Offred. Comments on themes and forms of expression and concerns will be linked to particular appropriate critical writing which will be further explored in Chapter 4.

These key issues underpin the themes of the novel. One of the truly important elements of this novel is the way in which it engages various philosophical and value related issues and enables us to engage with the contradictory, problematic positions which you can take in terms of these issues. It is not simply a matter, for example, of defining Gilead as an oppressive regime, since it also offers safety for women, but in so doing it forces collusion and punishes discontent and rebellion. Freedom is a central issue. Freedom in Gilead is freedom 'from' various attacks and threats, not freedom 'to' do what you would like to freedom of choice; so we might ask, what then is the nature of freedom? Telling stories enables a voicing of individual experience. It is of course itself an artificial construction, a performance, a way of making sense of the world and events by shaping and sharing them and Offred's first person narrative draws us in, filled with realistic details and emotional responses but she constantly reminds us that she is shaping what happens, making it up, making it manageable, telling and retelling to make sense, influenced by the ways in which people tell stories. Where then is truth? Language is also important throughout the novel since in the Republic of Gilead, much language has to be coded, constrained. Women are not allowed to read and write, and power and knowledge are kept from those who do not have the language with which to engage. The rituals of Gilead, which involve various persecutions seen as cleansing, are given particular names such as 'Prayvaganzas', 'Salvagings' and 'Particicutions'. There is a history to the engagement of dystopian novels with the dangers of totalitarian society and, like *Nineteen Eighty-four* (1949) and *Brave New World* (1932), they frequently explore connections between the state repression of its subjects and their thoughts and the perversion and oppression of language. The narrator Offred is labelled 'Handmaid' because of her potential to bear children. Language is coded, thoughts seem policed and all sexual freedoms have been lost.

WOMEN AND FEMINISM

The Handmaid's Tale is read widely on literature courses as a dystopian fiction which deals with the possible future development of worrying trends in the present, and as a book by a woman writer which explicitly deals with issues concerning women's lives and bodies. As such, then, we can read it as a contribution to the critical debate concerning what women write about, how and why and to what effect, and for which audiences. Women's writing is often recognised as focusing centrally on women characters, or taking women centred, different points of view and perceptions and dealing with issues which affects women's lives. In this novel we have a woman protagonist, Offred, with whom we sympathize (as readers tend to with first person narrators) who invites us to share her perceptions of events and her disempowerment in Gilead, a republic controlled entirely by male power or patriarchy and based on the value of reproductive capability. Here, women are initially of high value but refused the opportunity to read or make their own decisions, make choices of how to live and who to live with and are unable to own their own possessions and money. The novel is taught also on women's studies courses as a book that deals with representation of women's roles, constraints, gender, sexuality and power, the management and control of reproductive rights, feminist themes, issues and reading practices. In literary terms, it is also interesting to consider how and if women might write differently from men, other than treating different issues or similar issues differently (such as power and sexuality, women's rights) and this leads to thinking about the use of language and imagery.

In reading *The Handmaid's Tale,* then, we need to engage with concerns about women's lives, gender roles and performativity, reproductive technologies and controls over women's bodies through the experiences of an individual, Offred, with whom we become very involved. *The Handmaid's Tale* represents and deals with some of the experience of feminism and the women's movement (second wave feminists of the 1970s and 1980s) and so is a product of a specific period, the late 1980s. We might also be interested in how we might read it *now* in the early twenty-first century, a very different context to the one in which it was written. All these issues are important when we think of women's writing and feminist criticism in terms of this novel.

Offred is a lone woman whose ability to produce children makes her a scarce commodity in Gilead, post holocaust and coup, and it is entirely for the qualities of her body, her reproductive capability, that she is valued. As such, she is reduced to being a walking womb. She is called Offred because she lives in a household with a Commander called Fred, hence her name which comes from the patronymic – father or husband's name – Offred, of or belonging to Fred. This household provides shelter, food, her own room and depends on her to produce the child around which it can then function. This product would be handed over to the ageing wife, Serena Joy, ex-TV proselytizer for domestic bliss and women's place being in the home. A child would also confirm the Commander's status, and ensure the continuity of the human race (or part of it). It is a huge burden, and the Handmaids, of which Offred is one, are treated not as possible lovers or mistresses or wives, but as wombs, of worth only for their reproductive capabilities. Hence, they are not expected to care about the quality of their skin, for example. Being able eventually to persuade the Commander to get her some cream is a big achievement for Offred and part of the collusive relationship she has with him over time. Nor are Handmaids meant to care about themselves as individuals; instead they are supposed to dedicate themselves to reproduction for the good of the hierarchical totalitarian society in which they are surviving. In Elizabethan days a 'nunnery' was another name for a brothel so it is ironic that the Handmaids, whose entire purpose is to reproduce, are expected to wear the white winged headdresses of nuns in extreme orders, and long red dresses and red shoes which both suggest blood, and the traditional idea of a scarlet or loose woman. They have no opportunities for any chosen sexual activity – risking being taken away in a van by the Republic's secret police, the Eyes, and probably tortured before being sent to the colonies to pick over nuclear waste and die young. Their sexual activities are confined entirely to surrogacy, bearing a child for a Commander for his Wife to bring up. Atwood builds on this as a biblical historical practice based on the incident when Rachel, who could not have children, was happy for her maid Bilhah to bear them for her, after having sex with Rachel's husband. She also describes it as a humiliating, dehumanizing, unpleasant ritual, the 'Ceremony', in which Offred must lie between the legs of the Wife, who loathes her and this activity, and be fertilized. Offred, in her taped account, does not describe it as making love or rape; it is an act to lead to procreation which hardly needs her involvement except as a vessel. Women are walking wombs, controlled by their bodies and entirely valued by their success at producing babies as opposed to 'Unbabies', deformed children no doubt affected by the pollution and fallout. Ritual and ceremony follow the fertilization and birthing. The households support the Handmaids with food and expect them to do the shopping but no housework, and they are forbidden to have friendships, relationships or to talk anything but a kind of sub-coded Handmaid language of biblical responses to each other, praising the weather or the fruitfulness of the shopping trip. Beyond the households, the Aunts, ironically named since they are neither like caring aunts nor part of a real family, brutally train the Handmaids to be thankful for and compliant with their roles, enforced by curfews, silence, and some beating about the feet and hands (not necessary for childbirth, their only function) with electric cords should they disobey, try to escape, or undermine the training. This happens to Offred's best friend Moira, always a rebel, a model of alternative ways of being and the possibility of behaving differently in a tyrannical regime. Moira speaks out against the regime, declares her sexual choice as lesbian, and escapes. We see her again, having chosen to be in a brothel – the forbidden but surreptitiously legitimated Jezebel's – when the Commander, also breaking a number of rules, smuggles Offred out for the evening as his illicit companion, dressed in the outfit of a mistress not a Handmaid. In such a strict regime, which has removed all hints of sexuality and its darker side of pornography and sexual violence, women are nonetheless and yet again managed by powerful men and sought for illicit sex. In the early days of their illicit relationship, the Commander voices that old cliché that his wife does not understand him. At this point he only asks Offred to kiss him as if she meant it, and expects her to play a word game, which is subversive since writing and reading have been banned for women. Later, after Jezebel's, he expects her to have sex with him and, eventually to love him. But Offred has not chosen him, and it is hard for her to pretend.

The outlook for women in this possible future is indeed miserable, reduced to bodily functions and roles of Handmaids, Wives, or housemaids doing chores in the formal household system, or in the proletariat outside, as Econowives. In this critique of reproductive technologies and a dehumanizing control over women's power and individuality Atwood imagines a future which has reversed all the equalities and achievements of the twentieth century. These include the achievements of the suffrage movement which gained the right for initially select groups of women to participate in the vote in the US (1920), Canada (1917), Australia (1902), New Zealand (1893) and the UK (1918)and campaigned for various legislation for equal rights, equal opportunities, ownership of property, equal pay and so on. Women in the novel are reduced back to being owned by men rather than being able to own property, their own children or themselves, to make decisions about their own bodies and futures. In chapter 28 the turning point is seen. This is a powerful moment and a shocking chapter. Offred (under her real name, which is probably June) and her husband Luke, along with their daughter, are living an ordinary life when, in the course of one week, the President is shot, the constitution revoked, and armed bodies of Special Forces – troops of some sort – patrol the streets and control everyone's actions. This position in the future is contrasted with the moments of equality, hard earned in the 1980s, and the beliefs, actions and visions of feminists in that period.

Atwood critiques the notion of a supportive sisterhood. The women in Gilead and its microcosm, the Commander's household, do not have to carry out multiple roles – they do the housework or they are wives or they bear children, but this role separation, which might reduce the burden for women in an ideal feminist vision, actually leads to lack of mutual support, jealousy, performance, and resentment. The Handmaids do not necessarily support each other – Janine, for instance, is happy to tell Aunt Lydia of any incident of revolt among the Handmaids in training and to give anything away about Moira's escape if she can, and by so doing improve her own situation. She is referred to as 'that whiney bitch' by Offred and it is only in labour that they have any sympathy for her. Other Handmaids could easily betray you if you do not act in a devout and pious manner, so it is wonderful for Offred when she realizes that Ofglen also is only performing her role and duties and actually knows about an underground, a real potential for escape. Ultimately Ofglen commits suicide rather than be caught when someone, somewhere, not Offred, has betrayed her. Serena Joy only sets Offred up with Nick the chauffeur to ensure that there is a baby in the house, otherwise she resents her and loathes their enforced relationship. The Aunts with their cattle prods and Aunt Lydia with her rat's teeth, her rodent mouth, are not pleasant sisterly figures. The moment of change from the everyday equalities in Offred's life to the new regime emphasizes the fundamental investment in views inspired by feminism, however much of the feminists' excesses are portrayed ironically, criticized and shown to be foolish or excessively visionary. As Offred finds, she cannot purchase cigarettes in a shop because her bank card, the Compucard, through which all monies are controlled, has been frozen just because it is labelled 'F' not 'M' (female not male). We experience a terrifying disempowerment with her, and, as the job she is in collapses and all the women are forced to leave, no longer allowed to work, Atwood is pointing out – through Offred in this dystopian future – that it could be possible to revoke the legislation equalities and return women to dependency upon men's economic and political power, their good nature, their control. However this control is managed, this paternalism (caring fatherly behaviour or control) or patriarchy (politicized enforced male control and power often acted out oppressively) would in such situations take over from any equality, and be supported by the law, beliefs, perceptions and everyday behaviours. In itself this is terrifying to us now but for some women in other parts of the less free non-Western world, and for women suffering domestic violence and having no control over their bodies or their money, it is not a dystopia of the future – it is still a very real experience of the present. The book serves as a warning. One of the worst elements is the ease with which those newly empowered and those newly disempowered fall into new relationships and see the world differently. Offred, her right to work, own money, make decisions about herself removed, is thrown into a state of de-energized depression. While Luke says he will always look after her, this paternalistic response and caring is viewed as patronizing – he has the power, however well meant, he will now be in control whereas previously they were equals. She wonders if she is being paranoid, she isn't; the book isn't, she is merely being aware that all her power and rights are removed and irreplaceable unless another power steps in. Aunt Lydia later insists that the generations to come will find all of this – women's exclusion from reading and writing and rights – to be absolutely normal. That too is terrifying, that there might be no imaginable alternative and no power to try and make one come true in terms of the novel. We are assured at its end that Gilead falls, that Offred's testimony at least has survived, and that there is a more equal world. As a women's novel and a feminist inspired text then, this is neither simplistic nor blinkered, excessive or unduly negative. It points out the ever present potential for a reduction in women's rights, yet simultaneously it also points out the flaws in the feminist vision, and the lack of sisterhood among women. This sisterhood was once a claim of second wave feminists, of whom Offred's mother is an example. One argument of the North American feminists, whose views are remembered in a period pre-Gilead, was that against the dehumanization of women encouraged through pornography. The novel, however, is more equivocal, equating censorship against pornography with censorship of human rights and freedoms, and book burning more generally. It takes the campaign to make the streets safe and rape a thing of the past, literally, into an unexpected future enactment where such safety reduces all choice and sexual freedom, while illustrating how tenuous can be the hold on rights and equalities taken for granted now. Reading the novel in the twenty-first century we can have a more distanced perspective on the views of 1980s feminism, on the kind of outcomes they would never have sought, and on the ways in which (while they have many rights in the Western and parts of the Eastern world) they are frequently reduced to a state of disempowerment under extreme or fundamentalist regimes.

LANGUAGE, STYLE AND FORM. NARRATIVE PRACTICES

Margaret Atwood's style is diverse and self-aware, influenced by her imaginative and lyrical work as a poet. As such, her work is a mixture of the mythic and symbolic, the representational and the realistic, the historically convincing – whether such detailed certainty is trustworthy or itself a fictional construct. Much of her work explores the ways in which we construct history, identity, reality, and interpret versions of our lives and reasons for living. She focuses on the constructedness of narrative, the performativity of self and identity, and in so doing uses myths, genres, forms and tropes, and slippery symbolic allegorical names, locations and terms which resonate with the arguments of her novels. Atwood sees *Oryx and Crake* (2003), for instance, as a partner or bookend to *The Handmaid's Tale,* because of its focus on a dystopian future. In the later novel, the deadly BlyssPluss Pills lure people in an endangered future into believing they can have totally safe sexual encounters, while the excess and promise of the name of the pill belies its intent to sterilize and accidentally destroy the human race in the process. The language of the book suggests that promises or artificial lifestyles (including genetic engineering) are excessive and deceptive.

In *The Handmaid's Tale*, the term Handmaid is reflective of the religious fundamentalism which underpins the control of women's fertility and reproductive freedoms in a post-holocaust society, which has led itself to believe in military rule and reproduction of the dying human species as a sort of dedication to a new religious conviction. The Handmaids are the right hand of their male owners / employers and their infertile wives; maids in the sense that they are treated as servants, but not maids in that their lives are entirely concerned with fertility and reproduction. Language is tricky and deceptive. The Aunts are Fascist controlling servants of the regime who act like school matrons but lack any nurturing qualities. The Handmaids must speak in ritualistic language, giving away no feelings or thoughts in case they are betrayed by those who hear them and, if any radical exchange is sought, they speak in code to each other.

The Handmaid's Tale is limited by being channelled through the language and perceptions of Offred, the Handmaid whose life has been reduced to a procreative role and who lives in the house of the Commander and his wife Serena Joy. Much of the irony, the subtext, and the perspectives of the novel occur in the naming, and referencing which Atwood adopts to portray settings, events, characters, and ways of constructing the present. The novel begins in the terrible present in a school hall or army barracks, The Rachel and Leah (biblical names) or Red Centre (suggesting blood, power, violence, fertility), in which people, things and events are named in a contrary fashion in order to hide their purposes and deny intuitive or intelligent perception of what is plainly in view. The Aunts who rule this establishment are far from nurturing, they are prone to beat escapees and those who feign sickness to avoid the hardships, or to abuse them using electric cords and wires on their feet until the Handmaid's feet swell and they cannot walk. They torture and they do so as a form of control and normalizing which supports the regime. The Republic of Gilead is far from a republic, the name of which would offer freedom and equality. Instead, it is a totalitarian state whose rules cannot be revoked or rephrased. To deny the rule of the republic and in the Red Centre, the rule of the Aunts who serve it and train women to obey it, produces beatings and, at worst, extradition to the colonies where women pick over radioactive waste and die young.

An important characteristic of the language in this novel is the guardedness and the representativeness of the words chosen. While Offred must be extraordinarily careful of what she says, and tells us, talking in a form of ritual language in her role as Handmaid, some of the things she thinks when alone in her room, are quite at odds with this restraint. Here we hear from her as a person with a history which she is trying to hang onto in the face of the obliteration of her feelings, her individuality and her right to report and record. Language plays a big part in such obliteration or enabling. Offred and the other Handmaids are not allowed to write or read. Their language is controlled and their thoughts are meant to be equally controlled as a result, but for Offred they are not; as she finds the space and time to tell us her tale, so she recuperates a lost past when her mother was involved in 'Take Back the Night' marches and lived a hippie feminist existence, while Offred and her partner Luke and their daughter lived a life of relative equality with bank balances, loans, mortgages and childcare issues. These memories are delivered up as lost histories; what we regard as the normal and everyday has been denied and silenced in the terrible future of the Republic of Gilead.

Language is both a freeing and enabling device for Offred and a way in which to report the everyday and the historical. It is simultaneously a way of twisting and reporting, misnaming the truth. Names reverse the meanings of things: Prayvaganzas are mass weddings but are also about mass hysteria and crowd control of the women. Salvagings are also a form of control; they are not strictly about salvaging which is a form of rescue and rehabilitation, but instead about destroying. Those destroyed in the name of the regime are those who have been considered traitors to its values. A traitor is anyone with free speech who speaks against the regime, or anyone who does not or cannot fit into its strict rules about who is considered righteous and human and acceptable – so Black, homosexual, non-fertile women and anyone else who does not fit into the designed terminology and values is deemed worthless. Language twists and turns to follow the ideologies of its context, the value systems which colour and condition ways of seeing the world and so expressing thoughts about the world in which people live. Here it is no different – but Atwood's language and style can undercut the power of the totalitarian regime by setting Offred's story against the received versions, and by distancing the whole through a form of history – the discovery of Offred's recordings after the events suggest that at least her tale survived, even if inevitably, she did not. This indicates possible escapes for the reader. Intertextual referencing to Offred's tale by Professor Pieixoto, who lectures on it, and throughout her tale to the other dystopias from which this tale is developed, provides a set of spaces for the imagination of the reader to put the horrors of Gilead into perspective in terms of history, perceptions, values, and expression. (Intertextuality is the referencing of other texts to remind us of them and let their messages resonate through the text which references them). This perspective is partly achieved through the lens and language of genre fiction which mediates the very realistic detail produced by Offred. The genres which Atwood's text uses range from what looks like semi-fictionalized autobiography (Offred's construction of her life story, her reflections and memories) to dystopian science fiction to feminist text. Language controls the version of reality, the history that is passed on and the freedom to speak, and more importantly, the right to think. There are a couple of occasions where aunt Lydia mentions that future generations will find it much easier than the Handmaids to tolerate the controls of the regime. That, of course, is not only because they won't have the experiences against which to set the versions of these constraints but also because the language will have died with the experiences. The right to pass on information and the right to have divergent views, versions and expressions will have disappeared by then. Without any poetic or imaginative alternatives people will no longer be able either to imagine or to take the opportunity for alternative lives and futures. Language will remove this choice from people, thus disempowering them. As humans are language animals, this will disempower and dehumanize them. Atwood's use of the comic and ironic, and the satirical undercut and offer alternative ways of perceiving and being. Her use of intertextual referencing to other works and other times is a common element of postmodernist novels, of which this is one. Such intertexts offer alternatives, parallels, ironic versions, and imaginative ways out. Commenting on, introducing us to the language and names in this world, highlights the constructedness of the language systems which control it and the alternative language systems and versions which run alongside it, half glimpsed and exercised by Offred. All of this suggests to the reader that there are other ways of recording, experiencing, assessing and moving on from experiences detailed by Offred in the restricted code of the Handmaids. Offred's code is restricted because of her gender in the republic, where women are not allowed to read or write and where everyone has had to adopt and practise a kind of double speak, praising the unthinkable, celebrating the regime.

Offred the Handmaid's first person testimony is recorded, transcribed and then critiqued. These records from Offred are seen by some future readers as unreliable because written in the first person, and by others as trustworthy for precisely the same reason. They are a testimony to silencing, tribulations, repressions and life under a regime which reduces its people to their functions: control, reproduction, service, – and those who regulate those functions, Aunts, and various versions of the thought police. At one level, *The Handmaid's Tale* is also about the writing process. Offred comments on her own constructions saying things such as: 'Context is all', and 'I've filled it out for her . . . ', 'I made that up' and 'I wish this story were different'. Offred's habit of talking about the process of storytelling highlights the processes of constructing and representing histories, versions of events which are legitimated or re-expressed.

Language has been an interest for many of the critics of the novel. The work of Michel Foucault could be used here to explore the relationship between language, sexuality and power where Offred and her kind are forced into a silence of coded exchanges, and where surveillance predominates and only Offred's version of events can themselves survive her in a recorded piece, not even written down by Offred herself but transcribed later. Stripping women of their permanent individual names attempts to erase individuality. Feminists and deformed babies are treated as subhuman, denoted by the terms 'Unwomen' and 'Unbabies', while Black and Jewish people are defined in biblical terms ('Children of Ham' and 'Sons of Jacob'), differentiating them from the rest of society and so making their persecution easier. Thoughts must be veiled and unspoken and there are agreed, approved greetings for personal and other encounters, and those who do not produce the correct greetings fall under suspicion of disloyalty.

Atwood exposes the ability of language to occlude meaning, or to open it up to a variety of resonant interpretations, so it is fragile, filled with potential and dependent on who has the power over its control, just like human freedoms.

DYSTOPIAS AND GENRE FICTIONS – THEIR FOCUS AND CHARACTERISTICS

The Handmaid's Tale is a postmodernist text, one element of which means that it is a mixture of a variety of genre fictions and forms of realistic fiction resembling forms of history. References to *Nineteen Eighty-four* and *Brave New World* position the text as sub-utopian, or dystopian, enabling a critique and a form of warning about potential futures. References to religious tracts, most particularly the Bible, identify the Republic of Gilead as dependent on fundamentalist religious beliefs, used to code various practices and control human behaviour. Dystopias enable projections of the faults and potential problems of the present.

In one respect it is an autobiographical testimony from Offred who speaks it into a tape recorder which is later transcribed. In another it is a dubious historical record whose authenticity is itself questioned depending on whether you might believe it to be seen as a testimony or a reconstruction. To the authorities and Professor Pieixoto reading and discussing the text in the post-Gilead future, its authenticity isn't in doubt. To the reader reading it in the twentieth and twenty-first centuries we are likely to credit the text with being authentic because it is a first person narrative by an oppressed woman within the formulae which one might find elsewhere such as in slave narratives and testimonies. Atwood rewrites and critiques cultural and traditional myths, frequently using these to explore and represent histories and stories of women and men. Atwood takes cultural myths and investigates their roots, turns them around and exposes and undercuts them. Her use of irony and a mixture of the rich detail of everyday life with the equally rich detail of myth and metaphor make her works both realistic and fantastic.

Fiona Tolan (2007) explores the genre of the dystopia at length. Atwood shows that she recognizes the relationship of her own novel to dystopian predecessors by her inclusion of an epigraph from Jonathan Swift's *A Modest Proposal*, which he wrote in 1729: 'But as to myself, having been wearied out for many years with offering vain, idle, visionary thoughts, and at length utterly despairing of success, I fortunately fell upon this proposal . . . '

Tolan goes on to look at the work of Krishnan Kumar who in *Utopia and Anti-utopia in Modern Times* (1987) saw that since earlier days a utopia has been used as a projected ideal state, and an anti-utopia as a state in which everything or many things upon which one depends have gone rotten and wrong. These were both parts of satire 'in the early period utopia and anti-utopia familiarly jostle with each other within the same satirical form, often confusing the reader as to the author's true intent' (Kumar, p. 104). Tolan notes that utopia has a lot to do with 'questions of liberty and autonomy' (Tolan, p. 145) as does Atwood's own novel.

Atwood acknowledges the origins and influences of both *Nineteen Eighty-four* and *Brave New World* in her writing of this tale and the later *Oryx and Crake*. The influence of these two dystopian fictions is clear in the concerns of the novel – with reproduction and its control, with totalitarianism, identity control, policing of thoughts and actions, and a multitude of oppressions and constraints upon individual freedoms. Such oppression is frequently a fear in dystopian fictions which create a version of life taking to fruition and realization the results of whatever is currently in existence. Current problems and concerns are taken several steps further to their logical and dark conclusions. The early dystopian fiction, Swift's *A Modest Proposal*, suggested that a solution to the Irish problem of starvation under Protestant misrule, was that they might eat their own children. This logical notion was a product of his ironic recognition that England with its wealth and ownership of large amounts of Irish land, estates and grand houses, looked down on the Irish Catholics as if they were not human beings and so had no qualms about their starvation. Their Catholicism was almost as distasteful as their poverty and their large families were seen as abhorrent. Hence, the solution, said Swift (being ironic, of course) is to let them eat their children. This immodest and dreadful proposal was, like all irony, misread by those who it ironised. It was not seen as a clear indictment of oppression and racism by those who were oppressors themselves, or who benefited from the oppression. A problem of dystopian and ironic fiction is the intelligence, sensitivity and self-awareness necessary for full understanding.

A dystopian fiction is one which turns an ideal situation on its head, a utopian fiction where one imagines an ideal future with the development of all that suggests in the present society and then the development of solutions to all current and future ills. Utopian fictions project a situation when, for example, there would be an end to poverty or illness and perhaps long life and endless happiness. Utopian fictions, a product of the enlightenment of the eighteenth century, were able to idealize and imagine a regulated and obedient, clear and clean, healthy life but they were both a mixture of the pastoral, which saw the English and European countryside literally through tinted glasses, since pastoral pictures used a form of eyeglass to frame and tint the countryside, and a form of the projection of an ideal state into the future. Such a projection, like eighteenth-century landscape gardens, would be well laid out, law-abiding, conventional and harmonious without disorder or disrespect, without regret or dismay, illness or disobedience. Of course such an ideal world might well be also one without criticism and where all men are equal. One might ask about who is relegated to the position of second class and servitude to maintain such a harmony and balance, such an ordered society?

Utopian fictions are ideals. Like the perfect ideal city, the ordered life in utopian fictions are both disordered hells and projections of current issues and problems into imagined futures, so they are not merely the opposite of utopias. Aunt Lydia's version of freedom deals with an interesting notion which underlies utopias or dystopias. Lydia suggests to the women in the schoolroom that they have freedom 'from' rather than freedom 'to'. This engages issues around forms of freedom since that provided in Gilead is one of protective custody rather than choice.

One person's utopia could be another's dystopia as forcing versions of control and order might produce a pure and regulated state, but the force of this imposition depends on power wielded to control both at the start, and throughout. Fiona Tolan refers to the work of Lyotard in his essay 'Defining the Postmodern' (1986) where he relates utopianism to the metanarratives of modernism, and connects uncompromisingly with totalitarianism, wondering how any kind of mind might (to take a terrible example in living memory) think up and tolerate the genocide of Auschwitz as a way to ensure some utopian view of an Aryan future. This argument illustrates that in totalitarian states it is possible that there are atrocities committed in the name of a certain kind of ideal order. Such atrocities clearly indicate a form of dystopian existence for those suffering. In these instances, in arguments based on the work of Kumar and Lyotard 'utopianism becomes increasingly inimical to a postmodern worldview' (Tolan, p. 146). Tolan shows how Atwood has constructed her fictional dystopian world out of what lies around her, a very real threat. This is represented in her habit of collecting cuttings and evidence of the horrors of the current world. In the face of her work being called science fiction she has always claimed that what she writes about is based upon the world as we know it and on current horrors in some form or other. Tolan notes that,

> Like Orwell's reading of society Russia in *Nineteen Eighty-four*, and Huxley's critique of consumerist America in *Brave New World*, Atwood appropriates themes and topics from

her contemporary political environment. Evidence of this is found in an extensive compilation of clippings kept by Atwood at the time of writing the novel, referring to nuclear waste, declining birth rates, religious cultism, surrogate motherhood, and more. (Tolan, p. 148)

Utopian goals are idealistic but often the perfect state is under state control in some form and so they can be experienced in the end as a living horror, a dystopia. Atwood writes a version of twentieth-century dystopia and recognizes the influence of works such as Anthony Burgess' *A Clockwork Orange* (1962) describing the novel as a mixture of '*A Clockwork Orange, Brave New World and Nineteen Eighty-four*' (CBC interview, 1986). A utopian ideal of women's freedom from oppression by men can turn into a dystopian situation where the women have their identities diminished, belong to the men, and are reduced to their functions. Women in Gilead are safe at night from predatory men but the result of this warped feminist utopian vision is the reduction of women to their separate functions. In this Atwood undercuts the feminist utopian sci-fi works of the 1970s in which, for example, all women collectives love each other, live happily without men and enjoy intuition and community. Marlene Barr talks about women's utopian fictions as reactions to physical fears operating in the contemporary world where rape and invasion were everyday reported in the newspapers and on TV so 'the characters in speculative fiction's female communities would share the following reaction . . . "Is the world unsafe for women?" If so, they decide to develop a curfew and keep the men indoors' (Barr, 1987, p. 5. This quote from Barr is taken from E. M. Broner's novel *A Weave of Women* (1978)). Here the book burning incident in which Offred's mother is involved is read in two different ways: it is both an anti-pornography act – burning pornography, and yet an incursion upon individual freedoms reminiscent of the burning of books in oppressive regimes which would remove all forms of reading matter from those who are no longer free to choose what they read. The celebratory way in which the women burn the books is noted in the novel. They have developed a new form of exclusion and containment in their own building of a different future. One of the repercussions of book burning or magazine burning reappears later in the novel when women are forbidden to read at all, so that the Commander's little deviant activity with Offred is not illicit sex but an illicit game of scrabble. In a dystopian condition where silence, oppression, constraint and surveillance operate, rebellion and assertions for individual freedom can be seen in being able to leaf through an old magazine and play a game of Scrabble. This is an example of Atwood's irony but stands for the response against wider oppression which Offred and others suffer, where removal of reading and writing removes the freedom of representation, communication, and so of forms of thought and of power.

POWER AND RELIGIOUS FUNDAMENTALISM

Atwood's dystopia in Gilead is based on oppressive power, lack of free speech and enforced roles. In interview Atwood acknowledges that if there was ever a revolution and a totalitarian or repressive political regime following it in America, its form would be religious. Part of the decision to base the repressive government of Gilead on a warped version of the Christian religions and the biblical version of power, relationships and male and female roles, derives from the history of America's settlement. Historically, marginalized and victimized groups, those who felt themselves not free in their own country, immigrated to the US first in waves of settlers from Europe and latterly as immigrants from Europe, the Middle East, the Far East and what used to be the USSR. The biggest force of immigration was that of Transatlantic slavery which involved the transportation of millions of enslaved Africans to work the plantation economies of the largely southern states, parts of Latin America and the Caribbean, thus establishing a large initially enslaved, disenfranchised Black population in the Americas. Migration from poor or victimized Jewish and Irish, Italian and Eastern European people followed. But the first settlers were, in a sense, religious refugees. They both desired their freedom from oppression back home and to set up communities with a religious basis which were, ironically, often the most exclusive and rigidly ruled and controlled in the new world. This history explains the often rather odd mixture of oppression and repression, containment, control, and pioneering adventurous spirit which characterizes much of US history. Puritan migration and community settlements are of particular interest in *The Handmaid's Tale* which actually recreates many of the rules, regulations and indictments and chastisements which we can find in Puritan settlement history and the writings of Cotton Mather, the Puritan religious leader.

Atwood acknowledges that setting the tale in Cambridge, Massachusetts, was a deliberate irony. This is home to Harvard, seat of internationally recognized learning and therefore, one might hope, of free thinking and enlightenment. Harvard was also close to that other Massachusetts setting, the location for the Salem witch trials where religious fundamentalism and tight social controls led to scapegoating, based on mass hysteria and a prurience of imagination – sex scandals, religious scandals and social finger pointing, trials, and deaths. These were famously dramatized to represent the time of the McCarthy communist persecutions or witch hunts of the 1950s in Arthur Miller's play *The Crucible* which was written in the early 1950s and first premiered in New York City in 1953.

Atwood is influenced by Puritanism and other religion-driven regimes in her tale of oppression founded in the brainwashing of strongly held beliefs covering identity, behaviour, sexuality, and rights, and based on divisiveness and hierarchies which reinforce conventional divisions. She also had the contemporary version of such repression in her own experience. Atwood developed some of her reasons for writing the novel and much of the insight into repressive religious fervour and its dangerous repercussions in the course of her visit to Iran.

During this visit in the late 1970s Atwood was aware of the growing pressure upon women's freedoms by the political power of the Taliban. Women were described as protected, in a paternalistic sense, but denied education and expected to be veiled in public. This is an extreme version of the edicts of Islam where many women choose the hijab or headscarf as a form of freedom from being seen as sexual objects in public by men and deliberately prefer to keep their sexual selves for the home. Such a removal of women's sexual commodification from the streets, it can be argued, is to give them their own freedoms. However, in the regimes of the fundamentalists where the veil is not a matter of choice and education is banned for women, there is no freedom. Atwood witnessed this and in her speculations about oppressive regimes for women, merged the two, Puritanism and fundamentalist Islamic regimes. This might cause readers to speculate whether regimes fighting to safeguard their sovereignty have a tendency to oppress those whose compliance is necessary for their success – starting with women. Under such regimes, initially seeking compliance from others might well next lead to their Othering and expulsion or punishment. In Atwood's Gilead, those who do not quite fit the ideal – Black people, Jews, gay men, and old or infertile women, are all considered an affront to the tyrannically imposed 'normality' and face death or punishment.

Under the religious fundamentalist influences of Puritanism the women are named according to virtues, while in Gilead they are named only in relation to the Commander whom they serve. Offred is the Handmaid of Fred, the Commander. She has no name, she also has no rights and like the other Handmaids, if she survives she would be passed from house to house to bear children if fruitful, and sent to the colonies to pick amongst the nuclear waste if she does not prove to be fruitful.

The contrast between Janine and Moira illustrates the two extremes of response to such tyrannical control on women. Moira, whose sexuality is lesbian not heterosexual, and whose spirit is forever radical, individualistic, would rather choose the role of a whore in a brothel, Jezebel's, than to comply with the oppression of the religiously underpinned role ascribed to Offred and the other Handmaids. As a rebel there is some space for Moira and her existence keeps hope alive in Offred's imagination. Janine, ultra compliant, is seen as sneaky and collusive. She tries to play the social game to benefit from her childbearing abilities. In the event, though compliant in pregnancy, what she bears is an Unbaby. This failure tips her over the edge into insanity. Even those who conform cannot win in this society unless they manage to also fulfil the needs of the regime and produce a series of bespoke children.

Atwood's themes are interconnected. The dystopian form can expose ironies and oppression of any form of difference, or dissidence in an oppressive regime which prevents free speech, reading or writing, and reduces women to their reproductive and their service roles.

CHAPTER 3

READING *THE HANDMAID'S TALE*

This chapter begins with looking at some of the key characters in the novel, and then moves into taking you through the whole novel with summaries of sections and chapters. Here we look at the contribution of each section and chapter in terms of key moments in the text, for example, commenting on a chapter which establishes the situation in Gilead with regard to the history of the roles of women particularly the Handmaids, or a chapter which focuses explicitly upon the difficulties of expression and articulation under a totalitarian regime and the dangers of speaking out of line (punishable by death). The chapters of the novel are explored in order, although you will notice that some are grouped together where they continue to develop a theme or concern or a character. Chapter 2 of this book looks at the themes in a more general introductory way, and in this chapter, Chapter 3, we explore them as they develop through the story, the events and the development of Offred as a character. The themes, language or formal characteristics are explored in discussion of the chapters using quotation to emphasize points and some short extracts to exemplify modes of very close reading on the text. This chapter uses some close critical reading and referencing to developments in the rest of the novel and it is hoped that this close reading will provide a model or example in practice for your own engagement with the text.

KEY CHARACTERS
Offred
Offred is the first person narrator and protagonist. Her real name is never revealed to us. She tells her own story concerning

her life in the post-holocaust Republic of Gilead, the US, in the region of Cambridge, Massachusetts, set in the near future. In so doing, she gains the reader's sympathy, which is a characteristic of first person narrative. We naturally trust what she says, although her words are not a written testimonial but comes down to us from a recording discovered by a male Latin-American Professor, Professor Pieixoto, at some point even further in the future, when he scrutinizes her version of events as a part of his construction of and comment on the history of the Gilead period. First person narrative and testimony are traditionally both considered trustworthy– the events are retold by the one who experienced them, and problematic since when people tell stories and recall events they inevitably colour them with their own interpretations, selectivity and hindsight.

So we must and do trust Offred's tale but we also need to contextualize it. Offred's mother, a second wave feminist, was involved in 'Take Back the Night' marches and other activities. She burned pornography and invited Offred, as a child, to do the same. Her mother represented the energies of women in the 1980s who sought to argue for and achieve political, personal and economic equality while Offred and her generation reaped the benefits with their own jobs, bank accounts, and equal rights, at least ostensibly. This bred a certain level of complacency and comfort. The ecological disaster and political coup took place and a patriarchal fundamentalist religious based regime took over, establishing Gilead. Offred (as a fertile womb) is treated as valuable but placed in the security of the home of a Commander to act as the vehicle by which he and his older, sterile wife, Serena Joy can procreate and so ensure that Gilead has a future. Offred is one of many Handmaids who are treated as if they were half nun (they wear habits and talk in a religious coded language) and half prostitute, or, more appropriately, potential surrogate mothers since their economic worth is entirely related to their sexual fertility. Offred's tale starts with her being trained in a military type school, the Rachel and Leah Centre or Red Centre, along with other Handmaids. We hear of her life with the Commander, Fred; her attempts to make friends with Ofglen and other Handmaids; her seduction by and of

Nick the chauffeur, a dangerous activity; her own flashbacks and reflections on the past with her mother and her husband and daughter, their escape and capture and her speculations about whether either of them are still alive. Offred reveals and reflects on both the present in the Commander's house, the immediate past before she moved, then goes further into the distant past with her mother and her family. Ultimately, she seeks to escape as a van comes for her, but this could also be a trap. Offred's story is our only insight into life in Gilead, with some little documentary historical evidence presented by the Professor in his studies and speech to a conference, as a kind of coda to the book at the end.

One of Offred's main characteristics is that she is ordinary, neither intellectual nor rebellious, and the trials of her life are told with a mixture of calm detail and underlying anxiety, loss, worry about what the future will hold for her if she does or does not produce a child, as well as worry for her family who are lost to her. Offred's moments of self-doubt emphasize her terrible predicament, and yet, while she knows many of the other women in her position, including her predecessor at the Commander's house, have committed suicide, she is a survivor and does not plan suicide herself. Her resilience has been seen as a triumph of the human spirit under adversity.

Moira

Offred's more rebellious friend, Moira, is first seen at the military school with Offred. Under the strict gaze of the controlling Aunts, Aunt Lydia in particular, Moira cannot bear incarceration and control. Her energies make her a lively, more critical character than Offred, but also one whose choices constantly expose the violent controls of this regime. When Moira and Offred meet in the toilets they can have a few moments of quiet shared support, common complaint, a slight deviation from the tyrannical silences and order imposed on them by the regime. However, when Moira fakes illness and appears to have been rescued by an ambulance, it turns out that she has been caught and cruelly punished, her feet beaten, her spirit temporarily subdued. Moira's energies and need to escape are such that she eventually tricks one of the Aunts, and runs off in her clothes.

We see her again later in the illegal but covertly government sanctioned brothel, Jezebel's, where she feels she has found a place which is preferable to that of obedience to an indulged Commander or the existence of a nun. Readers admire Moira's energies and rebelliousness, but it is dangerous behaviour in this brutal controlling state. We do not know what happens to her in the end.

Offred's Mother

A second wave feminist in North America, Offred's mother has brought Offred up as a single mother and is an activist – meaning that she campaigns for women's freedom and safety to walk at night on safe streets, unmolested by violence or rapists. She is active in condemning both the dangers to and inequalities in the treatment of women, which range from the economic to issues of sexual rights and education, and focuses on the role pornography has in making and representing women as sexual objects. In this last area, she gets involved in burning pornography and seems to have been influenced by the views on anti-pornography activities by women such as Andrea Dworkin. Offred's mother is seen as energetic, lively, active, but also a little short-sighted and single-minded since she has not set up a home herself, lives in Offred and Luke's family home with their daughter, and is far from being a nurturing parent. Through the extremes of Offred's mother and her friend, Atwood can chart feminist responses of the 1980s and also identify some of the potential shortcomings of the movement which, for example, seems to have indiscriminately banned both pornography and magazines depicting models of women, defining all as pornographic, and applying censorship. Censorship is central to the debate about rights and equalities which accompanied the arguments against pornography and women's right to have control over their bodies. What she and her generation declaimed against and took ultimately for granted is all totally ordered in the Gilead period, where to some extent a few of the feminist demands – for example, safe streets, have been taken literally but at a cost of any rights at all, any freedom, any power to own money or one's self.

The Commander

Fred, the Commander, is in a very high position in the governing body of the Republic of Gilead. As such he has an impressive house, wife, Serena Joy, and chauffeur, Nick. But he has a childless house and Offred's role is to produce children, thereby confirming his position, and ensuring a new generation. As Offred is one of several Handmaids who have lived in the house shared by Commander Fred and Serena Joy, his wife, we can assume that he might be sterile himself since no children have been produced. The Commander seems to have been a bank manager and in market research, and he is not unkind to Offred, though he runs the gatherings of the household as a Victorian patriarch would, reading from the Bible, and expects her to fulfil the variety of his developing needs. In due course he not only expects her to take part in the Ceremony of impregnation, but to visit him covertly, and accept gifts of cream, magazines, all of which are banned, in exchange for playing Scrabble. As a word game, Scrabble is also banned for women, who are not allowed to read or write. A man of power, the Commander can undercut and deviate from that power and when he plays these games, invites Offred to his study (which is reminiscent of a headmaster's study) and finally when he smuggles her into the brothel, Jezebel's, he shows both how important he is and how power can ignore and undercut the very power which is his role to reinforce.

Serena Joy

Serena Joy, a former television entertainer, used to broadcast and preach messages of domestic bliss and the need for women stay in the home. Older, partially disabled, she lives with the Commander as his Wife, and as a Wife has the run of the house, smokes, wears elegant clothes, and yet feels utterly frustrated in living the domestic ornamental life which she once upheld as an ideal for women. Serena Joy hates the Ceremony in which Offred must have sexual intercourse with the Commander while lying between the Wife's knees, as her surrogate. She also fears the lack of children so, in due course, she plans for Offred to develop a relationship with Nick, the chauffeur. Wives in Gilead are infertile, ornamental but act as though they themselves have borne and own the children produced by the Handmaids.

CHAPTER SUMMARIES

The Handmaid's Tale is divided into 15 sections and 46 chapters, plus an extra chapter of fictionalized history labelled 'Historical Notes'. Each of the sections marks a stage in the development of Offred, the development of other characters and the narrative and themes. Right at the end of the 'Historical Notes', seemingly produced by Professor Pieixoto who is delivering a lecture at a conference on Gilead far into the future (the year 2195), we hear that Pieixoto and his colleague have themselves organized the tapes into sections. As this is a first person narrative, we tend to trust everything Offred tells us as if it were the truth, but such reorganizing and transcribing undermines our trust, as do her own comments that she is recreating some of her memories in telling us the tale, and is actually often telling it in the form of fictional narratives – romance stories, for example, so that the novel is a piece of fiction, claiming authenticity, backed up by historical scholarship, which nonetheless shows us that everything we are told – even by individuals producing diaries about their lives, as with Offred – is always reconstructed and somewhat fictional, because they are looking back, reflecting, shaping it for themselves and for any reader to come. This concern about truth and fiction, form and language runs throughout the sections and the chapters, as do the other themes discussed in Chapter 2. The roles and experience of women and men under a regime which emphasizes the importance of procreation and fertility and which maintains a tyrannical religion-based oppression to enforce social roles, ways of behaviour, language, and in so doing punishes, executes or banishes anyone who cannot or does not conform to their rigid versions of what is necessary. This includes anyone who is Black, Jewish, old, proved infertile, radical, pro-choice and anyone who talks against or undermines the regime in any way, however unintentional. Such oppressive control over people's lives, identities, thoughts and being is gendered, racialized and also shown to be corrupt, as oppressive regimes of tyrannical power tend to be. But there is hope, and it gradually emerges for Offred in the form of radical friends, such as Moira, who refuse the constraints of the regime, and limited opportunities offered by those involved in a resistance movement known as Mayday and the Underground Femaleroad, which movement offers hope that other choices might be taken in the future, other ways of life possible; it also offers some personal hope. Offred often feels dead but talking through her situation (if she does this at the time) helps her survive as does learning to live with the limited opportunities offered by other people's needs – a relationship with the Commander, and one engineered by the Wife with their Chauffeur to try and produce children, and coded conversations with a particular Handmaid named Ofglen. Under oppressive regimes the human spirit struggles on and survives. Each section develops the story of Offred, with flashbacks to the time before Gilead, her home, family, her radical mother, and then descriptions of the everyday life she lives, from her arrival in the Commander's house to her stealthy exit in a black van. To safety? Or punishment? The novel builds up a sense of the constraints of her daily life and some of its small hopes. It also lays out, through her memories, the ways in which the regime controls and trains people, manages their language, rights, freedoms, social roles. And through the flashbacks and comments about the past – the 1980s, a time closer to our own – it equally layers in some of the problems of the previous time, some of its complacencies and challenges, and some of the ways in which people accidentally, unwittingly, unaware, allow their freedom to be totally removed, or have it forcibly removed. There are contrasting scenes from then and the time of Gilead which suggest how some of the things hoped for in an ideal sense – safety for women to walk the streets at night (in a historical context of fear of rape and violence) have actually led to more restraint and control.

The sections are labelled to suggest their focus. Seven of the 15 parts of the book are titled 'Night'. In these Offred is particularly reflective; in the first she speaks from the dormitory of the training centre, known as the Red Centre, in which the Aunts, a cross between camp guards, nuns and mean teachers – are schooling the fertile young women in the necessity of their total obedience, other rules of the regime and the importance of their roles as Handmaids, a cross between nuns and surrogate mothers. While in this and subsequent sections of the novel Offred reflects on the necessity of obedience and constraints on free thought and free speech, she also reminisces about life before the Republic of Gilead was established. Life with Luke and her family, when she had freedom and equality. And she uses the quiet space and time of night to move between despair at her loneliness and isolation, the deprived constrained life she has to lead, and self affirmation, recognizing that she at least has this bare solace of her room, her memories, her mind, some version of independent thought despite the regime. The final section of the chapters titled 'Night' sees her stepping into either the dark or the light, but certainly into a van taking her away to safety and freedom or prison and death – we are not sure which. But since her story has come down to us and has been preserved we assume in the end that she was rescued and survived which gives the otherwise very grim and thought provoking novel a ray of hope about human versatility, tenacity and survival.

Other sections often have very ordinary sounding titles which betray the strangeness of their contents and the activities involved in Gilead. 'Shopping' (II), for example, sees Offred and Ofglen on their regular shopping trip to collect limited food rations and, because reading is forbidden among women, there are no labels and words, only pictures of supplies and food in the shops which are each named religiously, such as 'Loaves and Fishes' and 'Daily Bread'. While shopping they gradually move beyond coded responses to some trust in each other. This is the only regular time when Handmaids are allowed out; other times involve the ritual of mass weddings, all women gatherings around natural and painful births – 'Birth Days' – and public shows of hanging women who have refused to conform in some way – 'Salvagings'. The latter is described in a chapter in which the scapegoating and brutal venting of hatred on a man also takes place during what is known as a 'Particicution'. The only really radical activity occurs at Jezebel's (in part XII) when Offred is drawn into dangerously radical activities with the Commander, playing board games, dressing up and going out for the night.

The sections indicate certain moods as well as developments in the storyline. Within these sections the chapters develop the themes in each section, where all those titled 'Night' have elements of reflection.

I. Night

Chapter 1

The novel opens with three epigrams and a dedication, 'For Mary Webster and Perry Miller': Perry Miller was a Puritan scholar who taught Atwood and Mary Webster was an ancestor of hers who was tried for witchcraft and who survived her execution, which meant that probably she was a witch.

The first epigram is taken from the Book of Genesis and gives a biblical foundation for the society Atwood imagines and develops – where Handmaids act as surrogate mothers to infertile women. Offred, the narrator, is equivalent to Bilhah, Rachel's maid, and Serena Joy is equivalent to the sterile Rachel. The second epigram is taken from Jonathan Swift's *A Modest Proposal*, where Swift pointed out the inhumane treatment of the Irish by suggesting that their over production of children should enable them to overcome their lack of food since they could cannibalize their own children. Atwood caricatures both American Puritanism and the Moral Majority by rendering literal what is currently only theoretical in American fundamentalism. Swift borrowed the idea about cannibalism from his 'American friend' and here the Canadian, Atwood, suggests that her American neighbour has invented the New Gilead, seen as a prototypical model society on which to base others.

The third epigram is a proverb taken from the Sufi tradition: 'In the desert there is no sign that says, Thou shalt not eat stones.'

This either suggests that people could be condemned to total lack of sustenance or alternatively validates inward spirituality and truth rather than revealed doctrine that is, Sufism as opposed to Christianity.

The first few chapters introduce us to Offred, the protagonist and first person narrator, whose autobiography this is, which we discover later has been taped onto cassettes and talked through in her captivity in the Commander's house where she is a Handmaid. It also introduces us to the context and the problems of living in Gilead in a time in the future. It takes us rapidly through her constrained life, Gilead, the regime within which she lives, issues of sexuality and fertility, performance control and hierarchy over personal space and identity, roles and even free speech. A totalitarian fundamentalist regime is described, in which women are valued only for their reproductive capabilities and in which everyone is under surveillance as if in a police state and everyone speaks a coded language influenced by religious discourse.

The first chapter opens in the 'Red Centre', the Rachel and Leah Centre, a cross between a prison camp, a girls' boarding school and an army barracks; it is actually set in a girls' school gym. Here Offred, Moira and the other young fertile women are trained to become Handmaids by the sadistic, collusive Aunts, particularly Aunt Lydia who has rat-like teeth, constantly preaches against sexual activity and enjoys inflicting pain on anyone who questions her form of biblically inspired brutality. This chapter also introduces us to the play on words since 'Aunt' suggests someone caring but actually here describes women in the service of the new regime. This regime, we learn, has been set up in Gilead based on fundamentalist religious principles coupled with patriarchal dominance, brutality and an utter rejection and condemnation of any critical questioning or alternative way of life. Following years of total disregard for nature, coupled with the comforts of both capitalism and equality between the sexes, races and classes (to some extent), a political coup has removed or murdered the President and Congress. The coup followed the gradual devastation of the land, pollution, defoliation and toxic waste that led to increases in toxicity in America and a breakdown of sustainable ways of living as well as a breakdown in natural chains, including human fertility. In this context, we discover, becoming a Handmaid is the only real choice for one such as Offred who is still fertile, since older women and the infertile or radical are condemned to the Colonies to pick through the radioactive waste. The rehabilitation centre reminds them of school; they sleep in cots with flannelette sheets, as children do, but they are also regulated, as in the army, with army issue blankets. Here they can be trained to obey the orders attached to the new roles for them. Here they are aware of what they have lost and the end to all hope for the future. – along with the smells of young girls, chewing gum, perfume, and smells of youth, choice, sexuality, so that there is a smell here of 'old sex in the room and loneliness' (13) emphasizing the repression of their choices and control over their own bodies. They are not going to have a future in which they can make their own sexual choices and although they believe that they have some control still because of the worth of their bodies in this regime, we are told that this is self delusion: 'Something could be exchanged, we thought, some deal made, some trade-off, we still had our bodies. That was our fantasy' (14). We are introduced to a state of emergency, the isolation of the young women, the voice of Offred, a moment between the past which is preferable and a constrained future. We are also introduced to the slipperiness of language because 'Aunts' rule with electric cattle prods to enforce the rules, and the brutal guards are called 'Angels', biblical, avenging, with no hope of redressal. The religious language merges with that of relations, both ironically since neither Aunts nor Angels are caring figures here. The girls' names are repeated in the enforced silence – Alma, Janine, Dolores, Moira, June. The only one not accounted for later is June so we assume that this is the real name of Offred, the narrator. Offred is remembering her time in the Red Centre when she was indoctrinated, retrained, restrained and taught to be a Handmaid. Most of her narration takes place in the time after this, in the Commander's house, except in her flashbacks of memory when she is recalling the past before the coup.

II. Shopping

Chapter 2

This chapter starts the main period covered by Offred's narrative. It is set ahead in the future, beyond the time in the Red Centre, when Offred has settled into her life with the Commander and his Wife. Offred describes her room as sparse. Each of her thoughts about herself is influenced by both religious comments, religious language and by the personal. She needs to ration her thoughts and feelings because her life is so constrained and she intends to survive, 'I intend to last' (17). This is in the face of her awareness that the previous Handmaid probably committed suicide and the temptation to commit suicide herself. When she describes her room, her train of thought often wanders to ways of killing herself, since they have removed 'anything you could tie a rope to' (17). She knows she is worth something in Gilead in terms of her fertility, underpinned by the religious terms, the sense of dedication to a purpose, but there is a vacuum in her personal life and her freedom is constrained. She plays on the term 'waste not, want not' when she asks 'I am not being wasted. Why do I want?' (17). The room is like a prison or an army barrack room, basic, without sensitivity or individuality, resembling a college guestroom or a prison cell. Like a nunnery, or convent, it has few mirrors. Her basic everyday life is like being in prison; it is defined by religiously informed constraint, personal denial. And what she can do with her life is only ritualistic, involving wearing the Handmaid's garb with a wimple hiding her face and long skirts. Fashion is an issue that represents the constraints upon the body, and Offred's clothing indicates mixed imagery: red for blood or for a scarlet woman, white for the nun-like life she must live, the regimentation.

> I get up out of the chair, advance my feet into the sunlight, in their red shoes, flat-heeled to save the spine and not for dancing. The red gloves are lying on the bed. I pick them up, pull them onto my hands, finger by finger. Everything except the wings around my face is red: the colour of blood, which defines us. The skirt is ankle-length, full, gathered to a flat yoke that extends over the breasts, the sleeves are full. The white wings too are prescribed issue; they are to keep us from seeing, but also from being seen. I never looked good in red, it's not my colour. I pick up the shopping basket, put it over my arm.
>
> The door of the room – not *my* room, I refuse to say *my* – is not locked. In fact it doesn't shut properly. I go out into the polished hallway, which has a runner down the centre, dusty pink. Like a path through the forest, like a carpet for royalty, it shows me the way. (18)

Notice how her shoes are defined in a way which will preserve her, as a woman with a mission, rather than for enjoyment. In other work by Atwood the significance of red shoes has been that of obsession, sexuality, danger, adventurousness. This is denied here. These red shoes are just part of a uniform. The blood which defines the Handmaids represents that of child-birth and fertility. They are not seen as having any other form of identity except their use as child bearers. 'Prescribed issue' suggests army uniform or school uniform, rules, conformity. The white wings of the wimple suggest nuns habits, outdated controls, and are also there to keep the women from seeing and being seen. The clothes she must wear – red garments, white wings – constrain her sight so that she must look forward and cannot make eye contact with other people, which suggests the ways in which Handmaids are prevented from knowing too much, commenting at all, or being noticed as women, because their roles are not sexual, they are there to breed. Offred has no sense of ownership of the room, it is 'not *my* room' (18), and is aware that what seems like freedom, a door which is unlocked, actually leads nowhere since there is nowhere to go. She is 'a sister, dipped in blood' (19).

We meet the Commander's Wife, Serena Joy, who seems older, shrunken, embittered. Her role as a Wife gives her power but her power has been stripped by bitterness and age. Her sense of being trapped is shown as she paces the room, confined in a different way from Offred. The women in the kitchen, Cora and Rita, are defined as Marthas, and wear another uniform, a dull green. Roles for women are strictly delineated and hierarchized here – from the Wife to the Handmaid and the Marthas in between. Outside, beyond the house, are more ordinary women, referred to, as if they are supermarket saving specials, as Econowives; their fertility is unknown and their lives are lived outside the confines of the houses run by the Commanders. While all these women have specific roles within the regime there are also others who do not fit into the scheme of things at all and they are defined as Unwomen. They work in the colonies picking over the radioactive waste. Reproductive fertility and production are important signs of success in the republic for the Commanders and their Wives, most of whom are infertile, and conversations about birth are carried on in all the groups of women. Here in Gilead they have a particular resonance, since it is only through reproductive success that women are considered to have any worth. Babies are worth something, they are the key economic counter or sign of worth, and those women whose babies are stillborn or born deformed lose status. While the women in the kitchen, the Marthas are disgusted at Offred and the other Handmaids' roles, finding their entirely reproductive service as degrading, they too recognize the need for the production of children for the renewal of life and see the dangers of a sterile society. Households without children mean loss of status for the Commanders. Each household eagerly awaits a child. Here Atwood engages with issues of roles for women as she introduces us to households in Gilead where there are different roles played by women. This reminds us of one of the aims of the second wave feminist movement, namely that women should not be superwomen, be overloaded, be expected to play all the roles at once – wife, mistress, mother, hostess. Yet here in Gilead the achievement of some form of sharing of roles between women actually leads to, identifies with their separation, rather than sisterhood. There is divisiveness in this differentiation – some cook, while others act as mistress, hostess and wife and others produce the children. Those Handmaids who cannot produce children are moved to another house. Clearly the differentiation of roles is a kind of servitude in this new regime. There is also a lack of solidarity between women which would have surprised second wave feminists, who argued for women-only societies. In this regime women are separated because of their functions, divided against themselves and each other.

Language becomes a power issue here in Gilead. Offred reflects on teasing her husband Luke about word derivations and meanings. There is no play on words, no play at all in Gilead, as if language and the world views which it enables are completely controlled. Interestingly there is no word to parallel the masculine bonding word 'fraternize' (21) and here in the household in Gilead there is no sisterly behaviour or the kinds of activities which should accompany chatter. While Offred imagines some friendship and interaction, what she knows is that friendship is impossible. This is out of the question; there is no gossiping or sharing of bread. Then the shopping begins with Offred taking tokens to buy the basics.

This chapter establishes a version of the past which is lost. There is a loss of relationships, language has been metamorphosized to be used in the service of the totalitarian state; loneliness, incarceration and the wearing of uniforms reduce everyone to their own lonely separated positions.

Chapter 3

This chapter alternates between Offred's memories of a twentieth-century past, in which she had what we would consider to be ordinary freedoms, and the present, her present, set in a future time in the Republic of Gilead, post disaster. This present is very constrained. Going out into a garden which is owned by the Commander's wife, Offred notes how the wife ties up the growing flowers, 'it's something for them to order and maintain and care for' (22), perhaps, since there are as yet no children in the house. She remembers that once she had her own garden, a place of closeness to the earth and the flowers. At several points in the tale Offred mentions flowers, here thinking of bulbs and their earthiness and potential fruitfulness, later watching Serena Joy snip off all the seed pods, perhaps to prevent their transplanting, scattering and flowering of their own accord, perhaps to control fertility, and later smelling the night flowers which again suggests a hope of freedom. In the past Offred also had the freedom to work but here she is confined to a single role and her own bare room. Because of the national importance of producing children for the future, Offred and the other Handmaids have not only been trained military style by the Aunts, but their time with households like Offred's at the Commander's is considered to resemble an army 'posting'. Her relationship with Serena Joy, the Wife of Commander Fred, is outlined here. The Wives are largely infertile, run households, but spend their lives in rather trivial and repetitive, ornamental pursuits like stereotypical 1950s housewives, or middle and upper class Victorian wives, living in homes with servants. The Commander's Wife, like the others, knits scarves for the Angels, the ironically named fighting forces, although Offred suspects they might be unravelled again and re-knitted, pointless, unused, a way to pass the time. 'Maybe it's just something to keep the Wives busy, to give them a sense of purpose' (23), but in her reduced circumstances, with no rights or occupation, solely there to reproduce, Offred is envious: 'But I envy the Commander's Wife her knitting. It's good to have small goals that can be easily attained' (23). Offred is treated as if a necessary evil to be put up with and not talked to presumably because Offred's fertility reminds the Wife of her own lack, and having another woman in the home, additional to the Marthas, the servants, is an affront to her dignity and role. 'She doesn't speak to me, unless she can't avoid it. I am a reproach to her; and a necessity' (23).

She has had two previous postings in other houses which 'didn't work out' (24), in other words, there were no children. So this is an important third chance for Offred. One of the wives in a previous posting stayed up in her room drinking, and Offred hopes that the new posting might not be quite so bad. Offred recalls their first meeting, being brought to the door by a Guardian, a kind of military police presence, and being shown who was in control of the household by Serena Joy's ownership of the space between porch and house, the threshold she might let Offred cross. Her greeting 'You might as well come in' (24) is unfriendly. 'I want to see as little of you as possible, she said. I expect you feel the same way about me' (25). She limits Offred's freedom to sit or stand, draws the boundaries between them, the hierarchy, the power, Offred's constrained freedoms of movement and role. It is confusing to know what to call her as she is clearly acting as the mistress of the house. Serena Joy is a former TV evangelist and advocate of the evangelist programme where religious context is reduced to being a desexualized hostess and wife. Offred recognizes her as the lead soprano from 'Growing Souls Gospel Hour', a Sunday morning religious programme which was shown regularly during Offred's childhood. Serena Joy has the accoutrements of freedom including the run of the house and garden and has cigarettes – which Offred looks at with longing, because she is forbidden to smoke as it could harm any child she was carrying. However she is 'tired-looking' (25) and she has a look of outrage, she is no longer cute. In her previous role, Serena Joy spread the message of domestic bliss. She emphasized comforts, women's role as homemakers, and her demeanour was grateful, pious. Having watched the youthful blond Serena Joy singing on Growing Souls Gospel Hour, Offred recalls the way she could smile and cry simultaneously, both a performance and an image. Now reduced, her only options are performing the role of wife. 'So it was worse than I thought' (26) Offred acknowledges. Here is an embittered proselytizer of the notion that a woman's place is in the home, obedient, domestic, conformist and religious. Serena Joy has been taken at her word. Now she is incarcerated in her own home, limping, her ageing beauty, her role that of the controlling but sterile wife, is powerful and dangerous.

Chapter 4

Walking down the gravel path dividing the back lawn, Offred notices 'the fertility of the soil' (27) and half-dead worms which resemble lips. Chapter 4 focuses on sex and fertility, constraint and license. These dominate Offred's thoughts in a land where only fertility is important and sexual choice is denied. Gilead pretends to represent the ideal American way with its white picket gated house and clean suburbs, but here there is no free speech and there are consistent attempts to control free thought. Another army analogy appears, Offred's Commander is in his 'quarters'. This is a regime enforced by the military, using the trappings of religion to legitimate its controls, the language of the one religion which uses terms such as Angels, Handmaids, Prayvaganzas (an invented play on pray and extravaganza, seemingly a moment of celebratory prayer but much more oppressive and designed to cover up the behaviour of others); the Angels are the military and the secret police, the Eyes of God, are brutal. Much of this chapter focuses on the men who are not exactly in Offred's life but surround it, and control it through their powerful roles. Men 'caress good cars' (27) but only the Commanders and men of status are allowed access to women, which means that Nick the chauffeur, who is introduced in this chapter is, at least theoretically, denied relationships. Nick is a Guardian of the Faith, and lives over the garage but Offred fears he might be an Eye, a member of the secret police, who is there to test her responses. Nonetheless she finds him attractive. Nick is lean, casual, ostensibly unaware of his lowly status, free to travel in his role as chauffeur and free to wink at Offred, which is a punishable offence. She worries about this because although he could be attractive, he is off limits to her too and any act of this kind might mean that he is either a misfit, or maybe a secret police agent, an 'Eye of God'. Nonetheless, starved of love, she also imagines him physically and the order to 'think of yourselves as seeds' (28) both suggests her fertility and that she is only considered worthy or useful in terms of that fertility in the service of the republic.

As the novel develops, this form of service of licensed, hierarchically supported fertility is tested as Offred clearly finds Nick sexually attractive, although forbidden. Later in the chapter she and Ofglen, her shopping companion, another Handmaid, are observed and assessed by two Guardians, young men also forbidden to consider the Handmaids sexually, and she longs for some physical contact. In this role she has some sexual power – she represents fertility and procreation possibilities and much is expected of her, but she has no real freedom of choice or opportunity. The young Guardians are obviously starved of sex Offred realizes, as she makes slight eye contact with one, a form of forbidden flirting. Without the right to have access to any women at all, and with pornography forbidden and masturbation a crime, the Guardians will be lucky if one day they are promoted to being Angels or Eyes of God and then able to work their way up to marriage or the allocation of a Handmaid of their own. They are also edgy, sometimes rash in their actions and Offred is aware of a discussion between Cora and Rita in the kitchen where they recall a Martha being shot by Guardians who thought she was a man in disguise, carrying a bomb, when she was actually just fumbling in her purse for her pass. Such actions and other controls remind us of the dangers of patrols and checkpoints in Northern Ireland during the troubles and in places such as Afghanistan or Iraq more recently.

Hierarchy and coding are important control mechanisms in Gilead. Also introduced here is the hierarchy of roles and the colour-coded dress each kind of man or woman must wear. Wives wear blue, daughters are in white, veiled to emphasize purity. Marthas, the women who do the housework, wear green and are referred to as 'dumpy' (31). Handmaids are in red, emphasizing a mixture of sexuality (scarlet women), blood (fertility) and purity (the white wimple). Forms of transport represent value so that the 'Commanders of the Faithful' have long sleek black cars emphasizing their power; there is a dark, obscure, powerful aura to both the vans and their drivers, the Eyes of God, the secret police. Women are important in relation to the ability to produce children so special transport, 'Birthmobiles', takes women to births and their celebrations.

Language too is coded, with Ofglen, the shopping companion, and Offred acting as each other's spies, mouthing only accepted religious, obedient comment and response on their shopping trips. With her little pig's steps, Ofglen is a potential threat as she might well be a believer and so ready to identify any little slippage in whatever Offred says. Power over thoughts and behaviour, the language of others dominates the chapter. Offred's awareness of the sexual power of her own role emerges when she realizes how exciting she and Ofglen must be to the young men around them who are denied access to women. 'I enjoy the power; power of a dog bone, passive but there' (32). It is a sexual power based on restraint, absence and distance. The chapter emphasizes surveillance, power, and hierarchy.

Chapter 5

This chapter introduces us to other ways in which Atwood plays on words. Ofglen and Offred go shopping, their regular outing. The shops are each named after their contents and from biblical sources, so 'All Flesh' is where you buy meat but it references the threat in the Bible about 'the way of all flesh' (that all people follow a path which ultimately leads to death) and 'Loaves and Fishes' is reminiscent of the parable of Jesus being able to multiply food for a large crowd. 'Lilies of the Field' comes from another parable which suggests that lilies of the field do nothing in life but be beautiful – this is the clothing store, with it very limited range – while another store 'Milk and Honey' is a further biblical reference, taken from Exodus, describing the fertility of the Land of Israel.

None of these shops have much to sell, and the women are restricted in what they can buy by rationing as well as scarcity. Latterly, shop names have been replaced by pictures, since women are not meant to be able to read. Of prime importance is the production of children. On their shopping trip they see the heavily pregnant Ofwarren, who was called Janine at the Red Centre. She is suspected of showing off, but nonetheless is seen as 'a magic presence' (36) since all the women would like the achievement and status of pregnancy. Janine smirks.

Chapter 5 compares the freedom of the past with its dangers from sexual predators and strangers, with this constrained present, where women are free to walk the streets. But lives in Gilead are uneasy, fenced in, felt as constantly under threat. Offred lives in a town and suburbs without sexual predators but also without freedom of movement, entertainment, freedom of speech, any choice over relationships, any chance of self development, and any children. Remembering Luke, her husband, and her daughter, Offred contrasts her personal past in a homely setting, when she had her own bank account, with this world where only fertility matters, and individual rights and identity are secondary to the success and survival of the republic. She used to be able to run in freedom on these streets, only worrying about stepping on the cracks, a superstition which could bring about bad luck. She was also able to use the word 'my', representing her own choices The strangeness of the scene in the familiar suburbs is the more enhanced just because it once was a familiar place, lived in differently in the past, before the coup which established Gilead. The contradictions of the two ways of living are uppermost. Even the word 'habits' has two meanings – habitual actions then, and Handmaids' clothing now. 'I took too much for granted; I trusted fate, back then' (37). Defined by Aunt Lydia, 'we were a society dying, said Aunt Lydia, of too much choice' (35), suggests a kind of lazy looseness which led to the current constraint where there are no choices, only enforced behaviours. The dangers of the past are remembered:

Women were not protected then.

I remember the rules, rules that were never spelled out but that every woman knew: don't open your door to a stranger, even if he says he is the police. Make him slide his ID under the door. Don't stop on the road to help a motorist pretending to be in trouble. Keep the locks on and keep going. If anyone whistles, don't turn to look. Don't go into a laundromat, by yourself, at night.

> I think about laundromats. What I wore to them: shorts, jeans, jogging pants. What I put into them: my own clothes, my own soap, my own money, money I had earned myself. I think about having such control.
>
> Now we walk along the same street, in red pairs, and no man shouts obscenities at us, speaks to us, touches us. No one whistles. (34)

Offred's memories and views of the threats and freedoms of the past provide both a balanced view and an awareness that no change or development is simply an improvement; each culture change has implications, ripples which affect a whole range of issues in life. As she details the casual clothes in which she visited the Laundromat Offred also emphasizes that these are clothes that she chose: 'my own clothes, my own soap, my own money', based on her own earnings which now seems an unimaginable freedom which was linked to a sense of power. Aunt Lydia defines the idea of freedom:

> There is more than one kind of freedom, said Aunt Lydia. Freedom to and freedom from. In the days of anarchy, it was freedom to. Now you are being given freedom from. Don't underrate it. (34)

'Freedom from and freedom to' is one of the novel's conundrums – ironically now that women are safe they are also more restrained. An ostensibly paternalistic (kindly and fatherly) regime is actually one which is oppressive, violent, bigoted and set to deny and punish all difference, whether in thought, action or nature. That you can get used to such a totalitarian regime and the world views imposed by those in control, whatever they happen to be, is alarming and reminds us of other totalitarian Fascist states, such as Nazi Germany or Iran under the Taliban. This change of perception is emphasized when the two Handmaids, Offred and Ofglen, come across a group of Japanese tourists who are visiting the fundamentalist state and are fascinated by the Handmaids, 'cocking their head to one side like robins' (38). But the Handmaids are shocked at the clothes the women are wearing. Atwood emphasizes how freedom is in the mind and also the body, and how regimes ensure the normalizing of whatever their beliefs and rules are, though Offred and the first generation in the new regime are moving between the previous way of living to that of Gilead. They are controlled, repressed, coded. We notice how the clothes and make-up of the Japanese tourists is described as sexualized, offensively tarty, performative, while we, in the West and in the democratic or non-fundamentalist parts of the East such as Japan, see it as Westernized, everyday clothing.

> A group of people is coming towards us. They're tourists, from Japan it looks like, a trade delegation perhaps, on a tour of the historic landmarks or out for local colour. They're diminutive and neatly turned out; each has his or her camera, his or her smile. They look around, bright-eyed, cocking their heads to one side like robins, their very cheerfulness aggressive, and I can't help staring. It's been a long time since I've seen skirts that short on women. The skirts reach just below the knee and the legs come out from beneath them, nearly naked in their thin stockings, blatant, the high-heeled shoes with their straps attached to the feet like delicate instruments of torture. The women teeter on their spiked feet as if on stilts, but off balance; their backs arch at the waist, thrusting the buttocks out. Their heads are uncovered are uncovered and their hair too is exposed, in all its darkness and sexuality. They wear lipstick, red, outlining the damp cavities of their mouths, like scrawls on a washroom wall, of the time before.
>
> I stop walking. Ofglen stops beside me and I know that she too cannot take her eyes off these women. We are fascinated, but also repelled. They seem undressed. It has taken so little time to change our minds, about things like this.
>
> Then I think: I used to dress like that. That was freedom. Westernized, they used to call it. (38)

Then the interpreter asks if they are happy, and Offred realizes that she and Ofglen represent the hidden, the forbidden, as do Arab women from fundamentalist countries wearing the Hijab (veil) and the burka (face totally covered except for the eyes) when they are in a Westernized context. As the interpreters are likely to be Eyes it is important to agree that they are happy, and also not to appear immodest or allow themselves to be photographed. Atwood was influenced by her own visits to Iran and her awareness of the strict codes of the Taliban which prevented women from being educated, owning property, revealing their faces in public. She was also influenced by her research into the Puritan regimes in America and draws parallels between these two different totalitarian fundamentalist regimes and indicators to identify the sexuality of the individual self. Offred naturally oscillates between her projections of a constrained present and a past of warmth and freedom but, the text seems to suggest, already even her perceptions are changing and it will be much more straightforward for her in time, and for a second generation, to accept these extremely hierarchized, divisive and restrictive ways as normal.

Chapter 6

The novel is set in Cambridge, Massachusetts, home also to Harvard University, around which Offred and Ofglen now walk. Locating the football field, walls, turrets, bridges and the small church (the first one in the city erected by the Puritans) lends a sense of historical reality – though set in the future – to the tale and an ironic element since Harvard, as a great seat of learning and history, is here and now excluding women from learning and represents the stronghold of the oppressive regime of the Republic of Gilead. It has gates, darkened windows, and high walls and resembles a military camp, a walled compound, floodlit with an electronic alarm system. Prominent here is 'The Wall' from which hang bound and tied bodies, their heads in white bags. This is how this regime punishes dissidents whose full crimes we never know but which seem to stem from their former professions as doctors and abortionists (in a state which puts a premium on fertility) and their beliefs, actions, roles or accidental actions which define them as enemies of the state.

The men hanging from the Wall are all de-individualized, their identities hidden and denied. 'The heads are zeros' (42) and they are hung to warn others not to disobey. Abortionists and doctors are treated as 'war criminals' in an economy which sets such a high value on birth, although to Offred they seem 'time travellers', relics from a past when their work was valued.

Atwood is using Offred to remind us as readers that we are time travellers here too, lingering in their moment in the future. How you survive, Offred suggests, is through removing any response and acting as the regime would wish. She knows she should act as though she hates these men and notes that 'I must not feel' (43), since she might feel sympathy. Above all she is relieved that her husband Luke is not among them, this time. The really worrying cumulative effect of such removal of rights, and of the right to feel and disagree, is that, as with the manners of modesty displayed in front of the Japanese tourists, in time you get used to even the worst dehumanization and silencing. It is this which aligns *The Handmaid's Tale* with holocaust literature (such as the more recent *The Reader* by Bernhard Schlink, 1997) and works dealing with survival under totalitarian regimes. Inuring yourself against the worst, colluding, remaining silent, denying, ignoring, are all modes of survival in such extreme situations. Offred survives throughout the novel and her tale comes to us partly because she is not an activist but mainly because she maintains some sense of individual identity as a survivor in the midst of this bizarre, oppressive, contradictory regime. We see and have explained to us how mind warping, living with denial, comes about and is necessary to survival, but we also appreciate the more important and long lasting qualities of the survival of the ethical imaginative individual, someone who represents the continuity of the human spirit in the midst of necessary collusion, compliance and silence. Oppressive regimes partly control people through fear and partly through normalizing the otherwise shocking and unacceptable. 'Ordinary, said Aunt Lydia, is what you are used to. This may not seem ordinary to you now, but after a time it will. It will become ordinary' (43). A sense of the ordinary in which it is normal to be silenced, to speak in code, to be only worth anything in terms of a state managed fertility, and in which a whole variety of professional activities, misdemeanours and challenges or questioning of the regime result in death, is a terrifying prospect. Putting us inside Offred's stream of consciousness and her narrative, making the unimaginable real, are all effective ways of engaging us as readers. Atwood uses realism in setting, direct address from Aunt Lydia and from Offred, and a form of speculative fiction which runs so close to the familiar and the real, that its message is clear, a warning. The Handmaids necessarily collude to survive but Offred describes herself and the others as acting. They are performing, in an extreme version of the kind of performance of gender roles about which theorist Judith Butler (1990, 1993) writes; a control of clothes and bodily movements. Language also is reduced to set phrases, and ironic sounding labels. Mind, language, individuality and body are all controlled.

This section has introduced us to Offred, her constrained lifestyle in the Commander's home, the oppressive regime of Gilead and the broader themes of women's role, the control of language and expression, political and power controls.

QUESTIONS

1. What are the different roles for women and for men in Gilead and on what principles are they based?
2. How does Offred's narrative draw us in and interest us? Do you think that the diary first person narrative form engages us, and if so how and why?
3. Aunt Lydia talks about 'freedom to and freedom from' and compares the past with the present in Gilead. What does she mean? What kinds of freedoms have been achieved and what lost in Gilead?

III. Night

Chapter 7

In this chapter the gap between reality and language is emphasized, as is the gap between the past and present where once Moira emphasized sexual freedoms in her clothes, behaviour and academic focus on a paper on date rape. This sexual freedom is one from which Offred and others are now protected in Gilead. Through the memory of Offred's mother, the contrast is raised between censorship in the name of sexual equality and safety, and that which represses thought and freedom. During second wave feminism Offred's mother was involved in the burning of magazines and books of pornography. The scenes played out by Offred's mother and her friends when burning pornography and magazines which turned women into cosmeticized commodities was perceived as 'happy, ecstatic almost' (48). Offred's mother can be seen as dealing with issues of female relationships, of sisterhood, set against male oppression, and the demand for social safety of the body as pitted against the alternative demands of extreme fashions, for women to be constructed and valued only in terms of their looks and bodies. This society sets the market based flaunting of sexuality against the criminalization of male violence and rape which was clearly linked to such sexualization. Now Offred constructs such freedom to revolt against the oppressive regime of Gilead. In a sense, what Offred's mother has dreamed of and fought for has become a reality, since women are safe to walk the streets and their roles are valued. This society claims that the family is sacrosanct but has stolen Offred's daughter away from her and treats women as brood mares. Such a society is opposed to one in which women's body parts were imaged in books, and those images burned by activists. Propaganda, pornography and permissiveness are set against prohibition and patriarchal controls. The excess of permissiveness has perhaps led to excess regulation – not that the novel makes the link directly, but the reader does, since the text is composed of scenarios which are juxtaposed and which lead from one to the other, which emphasizes their connectedness and opposition.

Language is also an issue here since it is difficult to determine what is sincere and what performative. Offred makes her own personal references to *Doctor Faustus* (written by Christopher Marlowe and first published in 1604): 'Though this is time nor am I out of it'. Marlowe substitutes the word 'hell' for 'time' so indicating a question, a kind of horrible, deadly limbo state – one which in Offred's mind resembles her own. She wonders whether she ever understood what men said or meant, and for example what 'lie' and 'lay' meant. These words with their implications of both sexual activity and insincerity emphasize the power that language has on sex and identity. Sex, power and language are intricately related in this chapter, as they are throughout, and Offred's role as narrator, any narrative role, any version of facts and experience, are up for questioning since she acknowledges that even as first person narrator she is both constructing her tale and is aware of its artifice. She is making sense of her life and its implications with a specific focus and control over the events, dealt with through the slippery forms of language. 'I would like to believe this is a story I'm telling. I need to believe it. I must believe it. Those who can believe that such stories are only stories have a better chance. If it's a story I'm telling then I have control over the ending' (49). But she realizes and acknowledges not only that she has no control over the end of her reality, but that storying her reality constructs it in ways which it resists. It won't fall naturally into fixed forms of genre and narrative. Also, she isn't actually writing, she is talking. The dependence on any kind of record or narrative is both questioned here and also, necessarily, relied upon.

Foucault's theories of power, sexuality and the control of language are helpful in understanding the effect of the regime in Gilead, where coded exchanges replace reflection and discussion, engagement and decision making and where it is forbidden for women to read and write. The women of Gilead are valued for their reproductive abilities. Gilead places a premium on their fertility rather than their identity as individually motivated sexual beings, the kind of worth of self expression valued in the twentieth and twenty-first centuries in the West. As such then, Atwood brings together the main issues of power, identity, expression and control.

IV. Waiting room
Chapter 8
Power, translation and mistranslation of behaviour and clothing are uppermost in the beginning of this chapter where Offred remembers 'our sundresses and our sandals' (53), compared now to the cassocks forced on the hanged priests and clergy, the placards round their necks, the blood smile on the white hood of another hanged body – one of which they nickname 'snowman' – a childish term in stark contrast to the brutality of their deaths. The expression 'May day' or 'Mayday' (the international distress signal), enters conversation between Offred and Ofglen which starts a coded language between the two Handmaids. Initially, it just seems to indicate the weather, but is then linked to the French cry for help 'M'aidez' ('help me') which Luke had informed her was the origin of the word 'Mayday'. Offred's call to the reader, 'help me', is that of a trapped friend or colleague. Separation is one way of isolating and entrapping and she suddenly desperately misses ordinary family life, her husband,

newspapers and coffee on a Sunday morning, and has noted the loss of all such everyday occurrences now.

Econowives, who have lost a child, are encountered by Offred and Ofglen. There is no love lost between these ordinary women outside the households and the Handmaids, whom they despise for their supposed fruitfulness and status. Although Handmaids are the hope for the future, no one seems to like the idea or presence of them, and being treated as some kind of necessary evil is of little comfort to them. Serena Joy, the Commander's Wife, a mere shadow of her former TV evangelist, singing, domestic goddess self, also despises her. Pam, as Serena Joy's real name was, used to deliver speeches 'about the sanctity of the home', insisting women should stay at home – not that she followed this ideal herself (55). Her hair became more sprayed, her hysteria worse. Her car was bombed. Those women who argued for equality and those like Serena Joy who argued for domesticity were at war in the days preceding the coup, but now that her values have been taken literally she has nothing to argue for and is herself incarcerated in an empty home. 'She doesn't make speeches any more. She has become speechless. She stays in her home, but it doesn't seem to agree with her. How furious she must be, now that she's been taken at her word' (56) is itself a play on 'word'. The power of the word to be taken literally is Serena Joy / Pam's downfall. The inability of the wives to bear children gives them both a domestic hostess role and a dependency on the other fertile Handmaids; they are trapped in their own success.

Entrapment continues to be an issue as Offred scrutinizes the kitchen, considering the potential of the kitchen knife, clearly as a possible but unspoken way out of this oppressive scenario. In her position all she can offer the other women is a potential child, which they all want, and in this instance merely some oranges as she is the only one who is allowed to do the shopping. There is no sisterhood here with the Marthas, Rita and Cora, since 'I'm a household chore' (58).

This chapter focuses on language, power, sexual control. While Offred and her household are under strict rules and regulations, she can also imagine escape, through her memories of the past, and if necessary, through suicide. She repeatedly notes knives, sharp objects, methods and opportunities for to hang oneself, as if at least there is an alternative if she can bear her trapped life no more. The black market cigarettes, to which both Serena Joy and Nick have access, and the sudden awareness of the term 'Mayday' also offer some sense of the flaws, the cracks in this oppressive regime, and Offred can only start to think about taking some advantage of these. At the end of the chapter, however, something else enters. The Commander is seen rather too close to Offred's room, breaking rules, invading her space. She wonders about the potential for alternative values and behaviours.

Chapter 9

'My room' (60). This is all she really has but establishing her right to her room is a good first step. Sitting in her room, Offred reflects both on her sense of ownership of this room, her imagined version of a woman who has lived there previously, and rooms in which she and Luke used to meet in the past before they were married, where Offred could call up room service and indulge herself. The latter, a luxurious enough hotel room in which to meet your lover, is a far cry from this sparse room in which she now makes the most of at least being on her own and able to reflect. There is a contrast between the anonymous but free hotel bedroom in which they met, and being incarcerated in the emptied out space of the current bedroom, with its empty drawers and nothing which could be used for suicide; the scratches on the wall, the shatterproof glass.

Offred tells us she is trying not to make up a story, or tell lies, but this reference to narrative and constructedness reminds us that everything that anyone says or writes is shaped into a version, a story. We can never grasp true facts, but can only appreciate perceptions of them through what we are told. Offred, as our first person narrator, telling her own tale, is therefore both more authentic and untrustworthy since she will necessarily have to shape what she says about what happens, in order to make sense of it. Offred finds the message from the previous occupant, who we hear later did indeed commit suicide. 'Nolite te bastardes carborundorum' (62) which is schoolboy Latin for 'Don't let the bastards grind you down', a reminder that even in writing you can have the freedom to refuse to be controlled, however limited that is. Rita, one of the Marthas who work in the house, is aware, as we and Offred now are, that there is a resistance movement, 'a grapevine, an underground of sorts' (63). This chapter, although one of confinement, suggests potential for escape through writing, and through a community.

Chapter 10
Offred continues to reflect in the house and emphasizes that there is little that is allowed her. It is a house of little music in a time when songs about love are banned, as are many words in other songs since, for example, even the words to the religious African-American gospel song *Amazing Grace* are banned because the word 'free' appears. She oscillates between the heat of the house, speculating about Nick the chauffeur who is washing the car below, and remembering Aunt Lydia's condemnation of the licence of the past. Aunt Lydia, the most brutal and repressed of the Aunts in the Rachel and Leah, or the Red Centre, seems to equate bare legs and sun cream with the dangers of what she called 'Things' – meaning sexuality, sexual attraction. But she clearly both condemns and jealously resents the relationships others had in the past. Offred emphasizes this resentment in the rather cruel image of Aunt Lydia crying, then showing her 'mouth of a dead rodent' (65), her rats' teeth. Prior to their incarceration in the Red Centre for training as Handmaids, Offred and Moira's sexual freedoms involved smoking, and joking about giving underwear/'underwhore' parties. This was freedom to be an individual in control of their own sexuality, a freedom completely denied by the regime, and by controlling women such as Aunt Lydia. For feminist readers, this chapter exposes a lack of sisterhood among women, which Atwood explores at length in her later novels *Cat's Eye* (1988) and *The Robber Bride* (1993). Aunt Lydia, with her cattle prod and frustrations, is a collusive part of a regime which refuses women freedom over their own bodies and consigns their sexual practice to legitimated procreation for the future of Gilead. There is safety for women in Gilead, and censorship of the freer but often more pornographic, sadistic, side of sexual freedom which, it was argued, led to the 'Pornomarts', rapes and murders, a dangerous lack of law and control (as defined in this regime),

where 'there were stories in the newspapers, of course, corpses in ditches or the woods, bludgeoned to death or muti- lated, interfered with as they used to say' (66). However, any kind of sexual choice is forbidden in Gilead where there is a completely regimented lack of any freedom of choice. In the past, Offred's freedoms were many, and ordinary, taken for granted. She even indulged in the childish prank of throwing water bombs out of the bedroom windows with Moira.

This chapter points out the differences between freedom and incarceration and constraint; between regulation of the truly dangerous, and total censorship. It identifies the poten- tial for initially well meaning curtailment of sexual license which produced titillation but also fuelled violence, to develop into oppressive censorship and denial of freedom of thought, speech, and action. The regulation of the individual goes beyond the sexual. Women are forbidden to read and to develop and share ideas. Offred finds the cushion with the religious (but still banned) word 'Faith', written and sewn in needlepoint. Freedom, which you take for granted, is also expressed in writing, in the space between what's officially written. Offred comments, 'we lived, as usual, by ignoring. . . . We lived in the blank white spaces at the edges of print' (66). This emphasizes the importance of writing, storytelling, and Offred's own way of staying sane, reflecting on the past and telling her story to an audience she does not know exists, but must trust will one day read her words.

Chapter 11

Under extreme control, there is always power and licence which emerges from a crack in the system. In this chapter Offred's value as producer of babies is uppermost as she is taken for her regular check up to the gynaecologist with the hope that she, being a fertile woman, will conceive. This trip, 'obligatory', is compared to any previous, voluntary visits to the doctor. The symbolism of snakes and swords of the past represent qualifications and oaths as a physician, but also stand for surveillance and control in Gilead. However, the doctor, with his ultimate power over the most valuable item in this society, a fertile woman, uses and misuses his own authority. He both treats Offred as an object, examining only her torso masked in white gauze, and offers to service her sexually, addressing her in a sleazy voice as in a third rate movie, as 'honey' (70). Since the Commander might in fact be 'sterile', another banned word, this could be Offred's only route to pregnancy and so the fulfilment of her social duty, and the maintenance of some sort of social status. 'It's the choice that terrifies me. A way out, a salvation' (71) expressed in biblical terms but frightening, as to be caught would mean death. Sex is controlled by power, and in a totalitarian regime, there are always those who can undermine the roles because of their own positions of power. The Commander is the main example, as Offred discovers later.

Chapter 12

In the next few chapters Offred's body, her fertility and her role are uppermost, but so is her need to remember her past life and to assert her right to at least individual free thought. The bath, both a requirement and a luxury, gives her time to reclaim her body before she literally composes herself for the meal with the Commander and his Wife, followed by the ritual of an attempt to impregnate her, the 'Ceremony' which is detailed in the next chapter. She is aware of herself as playing a role, a part, performing. 'My self is a thing I must now compose, as one composes a speech' (76). This is one of many comments throughout the novel which equates authenticity or inauthenticity of the self, performance, with the ability to speak, write, articulate, each of which are forbidden to women in this regime. We also find out more about Offred's daughter and a moment in a supermarket where a woman tried to steal her, a terrifying incident which at the time she thought was isolated but would, in the Republic of Gilead be indicative of how much children are worth to an infertile society. Trying to keep a sense of her own identity is helped by remembering both her daughter, who she hopes is not a ghost and is still alive, and her past life as a family with Luke, her mother, in their ordinary existence.

This section, 'waiting room', explores Offred's situation further, her opportunities for reflection, her sense of trying to place herself, maintain her identity in a limited, constrained role and space. It provides the reader with a useful amount of back story about Offred's family, her child and husband, her free life before the republic and her current constrained role. It emphasizes how Offred is a woman in waiting, waiting to bear a child, waiting for something to happen to her.

QUESTIONS

1. What do we find out about Offred's previous freedoms with Luke, her family and with her friend Moira in contrast to her current constrained role?
2. What issues are raised in this section concerning freedom and control, in terms of speech, rights, and sexual activity? How are they expressed, and explored?
3. How do the various plays on words, the codes and restraints on language and expression operate in Gilead and how do they enable and prevent Offred from exploring and expressing her feelings?

V. Nap
Chapter 13

' . . . the long parentheses of nothing. Time as white sound'
(79)

Boredom and blank time are a feature of this chapter in which Offred also remembers time at the Red Centre where Moira's non-conformist behaviour offers an alternative to the status and obedience enforced by the Aunts. The Aunts treat the young women as mothers in waiting. They insist on napping in the afternoon, getting used to having nothing to do, since like the animals and birds used in psychology experiments with which Offred compares them, these Handmaids in the making are reduced to their functions and given no freedom of choice, no free space to think. Like the pigeons in the random sample, should they speculate that a reward might eventually come when there is nothing but an experiment going on, they could easily spend all their energies hopelessly hoping, pecking themselves to death. At this point Offred seems to be suggesting putting up with this, and that the lack of the opportunities to make decisions, to act, to develop and hope is better managed in a kind of stupor of conformity, is little more than bed rest. Offred remembers paintings in harems which suggested the same kind of endless waiting: 'paintings about suspended animation; about waiting, about objects not in use. They were paintings about boredom' (79).

Set against this deadening conformity, however, are Moira's constant radical energies, her talking through the keyhole in the toilets, her wearing of red shoes, (always a symbol of energy, sexuality, power and danger in Atwood's novels and short stories). The memories of life before the Red Centre and suggestions of escape all offer an imaginative alternative. Moira is not afraid to compare their condition with that of being incarcerated in an insane asylum. She's a radical thinker. She does not merely comply, she can take a critical stance, but within the confines of the novel the only final way out for Moira is to be sent to work in a brothel, Jezebel's where Offred later meets her, where her radical sexual energies are exploited and managed. Possibly another future is that of escaping through the underground, but that seems unlikely.

We also see more of Janine, who in the Testifying moment of the day at the Red Centre tells the tale of being gang raped at 14 and having an abortion. Janine is an attention seeker who likes to comply. A group chant follows which directly blames her for her bad experiences and it appears that she needs to be seen as guilty as well as a victim. She is reduced to looking sad, weepy, and it is in her treatment as a cry baby who deserved such cruelty that there is further indication of the lack of sisterhood in this women-only community of sorts. Atwood's exploration of the women-only community focuses on fertility and obedience, emphasizing the cruelties of women to each other, and the complicity based on a sexual pecking order rather than any solidarity. This is further evidence of how unpleasant the achievement of a women's community could be, in the wrong circumstances, based on such values and constraint as this one is in Gilead. Spite and bullying predominate, sisterhood is absent. It is no feminist ideal.

Offred, resting, focuses on the past with Luke, and remembers trying to rescue her daughter when they escaped from the beginning of the effects of the disastrous coup, attempting to cross the borders between the US and Canada, and avoid the regime. She was helpless in the face of force and numbers and remembers events, but only as a dream. 'I can see her, going away from me, through the trees which are already turning, red and yellow, holding her arms out to me, being carried away' (85). It is a dream memory, a sequence of loss, the colours of autumn emphasizing the end of her days as part of a family unit, suggesting winter to come. Offred's imagination and memory keep her focused and sane, while her body, used to control her, her only item of value, is also ambiguous. It is her only worth in the economy of this regime, used against her, yet, as she claims and reclaims it as her own, this gives her power again, power which along with memory, telling her tale and imagining alternatives suggests hope at least for the spirit of humanity in adversity – in Offred's case, of one trapped in a totalitarian, fundamentalist regime.

Although she states 'I wait, washed, brushed, fed, like a prize pig' (79) ready to be used in the regime to produce children, she nevertheless feels her body is also her own:

I sink down into my body as into a swamp, fenland, where only I know the footing. Treacherous ground, my own territory. I become the earth I set my ear against, for rumours of the future. Each twinge, each murmur of slight pain, ripples of sloughed-off matter, swellings and diminishing of tissue, the droolings of the flesh, these are signs, these are the things I need to know about. Each month I watch for blood, fearfully, for when it comes it means failure. I have failed once again to fulfil the expectations of others, which have become my own.

I used to think of my body as an instrument, of pleasure, or a means of transportation, or an implement for the accomplishment of my will. I could use it to run, push buttons, of one sort or another, make things happen. There were limits but my body was nevertheless lithe, single, solid, one with me. (83–4)

The language here suggests Offred's body is like a swamp, both 'treacherous ground', and 'my own territory' (83). She is like 'the earth', like the unnamed woman in her earlier novel,

Surfacing (1972), who also sank down and tried to become one with the earth and nature and who used this transitional state as one to work her way back to a sense of wholeness of self. It used to be 'an instrument, of pleasure' (83), to move within, and to use, something in the control of her own will. But now she feels both that others control her body and that her body is somehow controlling her. In the past her body was at least 'single, solid, one with me' (84) and now it often operates against her, untrustworthy, in the service of the plans of others and not fulfilling their expectations if it does not produce a child. This experience of mind and body split is disorientating, problematic. All she is, is a vehicle for child production, to hold and nurture a fertilized egg.

> Now the flesh arranges itself differently. I'm a cloud, congealed around a central object, the shape of a pear, which is hard and more real than I am and glows red within its translucent wrapping. Inside it is a space, huge as the sky at night and dark and curved like that, though black-red rather than black. Pinpoints of light swell, sparkle, burst and shrivel within it, countless as stars. Every month there is a moon, gigantic, round, heavy, an omen. It transits, pauses, continues on and passes out of sight, and I see despair coming towards me like famine. To feel that empty, again, again. I listen to my heart, wave upon wave, salty and red, continuing on and on, marking time. (84)

The moon is her ovulation, the egg, and when there is no fertilization she is emptied out again, aligned with the waves which are also controlled by the process of the moon and, in her case, merely 'marking time'.

QUESTIONS

1. How does Atwood represent the relationships between women in these chapters?
2. What images and metaphors are being used here to indicate the ways in which Offred feels controlled by her role as producer of children? Why are these images and metaphors being used?

VI. Household

Chapter 14

Although this section and group of chapters is labelled 'household', it also focuses on the ways in which power operates on a political as well as on a personal, local front.

This chapter mostly takes place in the sitting room where Serena Joy, Offred, the Marthas and Nick gather, a parody of a Victorian family awaiting the Commander, who is always late, to read them the Bible, which emphasizes his power, not least since none of the women are allowed to read or write. This Bible reading practice was one familiar in Victorian households where servants were often kept in ignorance; education has been banned as a feature of many totalitarian states in the same way. Knowledge is power and reading and writing might spread debate or dissidence. Indeed, Offred telling us her tale not only informs us about her life but warns more generally about the collusive, all encompassing power of regimes which take away power from others, deny freedoms, impose regimentation and rituals and live by suppressing the truth, spreading lies, and scapegoating others as the enemy.

This room, meticulously described, is a faded, outdated construction of a certain aged genteel version of femininity and money (though Offred believes the 'family portraits' on the walls to be of fake construction – Serena Joy's attempts at claiming heritage and history). The room represents 'one of the shapes money takes when it freezes' (89). Serena Joy's tastes are hard, acquisitive like the Commander's thumbs while pretending to be fragile and feminine, and are faded and outdated. 'The tastes of Serena Joy are a strange blend: hard lust for quality, soft sentimental cravings' (90). Offred has adopted the values of the time and place, characterizing Serena Joy in terms of her fertility as well as her flowers as 'withered' (91). The Lily of the Valley perfume (something worn by one's grandmother and bought by small children) emphasizes the dated performance of a Victorian or Edwardian household, which resonates with the powerful control of Serena's tastes and the power of the Commander – that over the word, over their roles, a power he seems to both enjoy, feel tired about and, later we discover, undermines by deviating from the strict rules. His ownership and control is like a marriage emphasized through wordplay. '*Household*: that is what we are. The Commander is the head of the household. The house is what he holds. To have and to hold, till death do us part' (91). The pretend family are also gathered for the news, which Serena Joy allows them to see, illicitly, wielding her own power. What they see reminds us of George Orwell's dystopian novel *Nineteen Eighty-four* which along with Aldous Huxley's earlier *Brave New World* are major influences on the novel.

In Orwell's *Nineteen Eighty-four* Winston Smith, a civil servant, becomes tired of falsifying the news, changing details on who is fighting whom, altering and erasing history to represent a version which suits the Party. Unlike Offred, he becomes an activist and a dissident, but like Offred he is alert to the power of propaganda, the political lies blatantly told on the television and through journalistic reports; in his day this takes place under the scrutiny of 'Big Brother' who resembles the Eyes, the secret police in *The Handmaid's Tale*. Manipulation and control of the police is managed partly through reproductive technologies in *Brave New World*, as it is for Offred and the population of Gilead. So here Atwood intertextually references these two powerful dystopian novels and places the problem situation in just post contemporary US, a nation which has never been invaded, has provided homes for religious sects and dissidents, prides itself on free speech and on individual human rights but is, she suggests here, equally vulnerable to takeover and misrepresentation, tyranny through the imposition of the values and rules of such a regime. This is emphasized in the news. Alternative versions of the present are censored out with the blockage of the Montreal satellite station's versions of news, just as in some countries the Arab world's versions of events in Iran, Iraq, Afghanistan and elsewhere are only available on Al Jazeera, wherever it can be tuned into, while other versions, quite different from those of Al Jazeera, are available in the US. Different regimes tune out the versions of the other; this selectivity offers a limited perspective on events and coverage is biased by the absence of alternatives. In this war, religious groups fight and send refugees. The novel of course was written before 9/11 and the attack on the twin towers of Wall Street, so for the first time in history, the war has come to the US. The US is not used to seeing images of refugees in its own land, and the displacement of groups of current citizens with the large-scale population movement of African Americans or 'Sons of Ham' to Detroit (Offred can't imagine how) and to the 'National Homelands' (93) in Dakota, presumably to farm, are all a grim surprise and warning that no place is immune from the evils of politics in practice. All these transplantings of people echo the kind of movements of displaced persons, mass refugees, across central and Eastern Europe, across Afghanistan, Iraq and the Middle East (some of these since the publication of this novel).

The war is religious. 'The Appalachian Highlands, says the voice-over, where the Angels of the Apocalypse, Fourth Division, are smoking out a pocket of Baptist guerrillas, with support from the Twenty-first Battalion of the Angels of Light' (92). To the readership the idea of everyday religious groups smoking each other out, calling each other 'Angel' when wielding deadly power is most terrifying and absurd. That those watching the TV are only shown victories, the frightened bruised faces of the defeated Quakers and the breaking up of an underground ring, emphasizes the control of the truth, the mediation by propagandist TV and news. Offred feels she must hide her own name for self-protection, to keep something of her former self in her own care. 'I keep the knowledge of this name like something hidden, some treasure I'll come back to dig up, one day' (94). This suggests the need to preserve identity, to collude in order to survive and hope for a future. Offred's own memories follow this scene, recollections of the attempted escape with Luke and her daughter across the border into Canada. The fear, the false enthusiasm, the false passports, the sleeping pill to ensure her daughter would not give them away are all tales told by survivors of invasions, but for Offred the end was less satisfying. She believes her daughter is possibly dead, although she also believes that she may have been re-homed with a family desperate for children. She hopes Luke is alive, but constantly expects to see him hanging on the wall with a hood on his head. Not knowing is painful, collusion with the tyranny of thought and action are constant and demoralizing: 'white, flat, thin. I feel transparent . . . I'm made of smoke, as if I'm a mirage, fading before their eyes' (95). But Moira's comments are there in her mind acting as a radical alternative energy. '*Don't think that way,* Moira would say. *Think that way and you'll make it happen*' (95).

Chapter 15

The Commander and the 'Ceremony' dominate this chapter. He seems to be part museum guard in a black uniform, part Midwestern banking president or someone who has worked in marketing, part shoemaker in a fairytale – able to play a role, perform duties. Being able to imagine him as ordinary and as part of a fairytale allows Offred to manage her response to him and his power. The novel has been seen as largely focusing on the constraints on women, under a potential regime, on the domination of women's bodies and the way treating women only as bodies controls them to the exclusion of any other aspect. However, there is also awareness and compassion for the constrained role men must play in this society, even though they clearly have more power than the women. We are shown that they are constantly being watched, much is expected of them and they must live up to these expectations, both in terms of power and sexual prowess. So 'to be a man, watched by women' (98) is a constant test of the Commander's manhood, his ability to perform sexually, described in graphic but not erotic or amusing detail, as if he had a 'tentacle, his delicate stalked slug's eye' (98) blindly moving forward, shrivelling back – dehumanized, like a creature, not part of a person. He too, in this description, is reduced to the level of his sexual performance as procreator of the next generation. His power is emphasized as he chooses the pages of the Bible to read. 'He's like a man toying with a steak' (99) suggesting life over death even in the mundane, and his power is also over language, like God, a specific comparison 'he has the word. How we squandered it, once' (99). This ceremony before the ceremony, or sexual act between the Commander and Offred, is a mess of emotions. Offred thinks of Moira and her attempts at freedom. Serena Joy muffles her crying, trying to preserve her dignity; an inappropriate response described in amusing ironic terms which bring the whole absurdity of the Ceremony down to earth, 'like a fart in church' (101).

But the potential for brutality for those who believe they can reject this kind of ritual, the whole regime and its control is emphazised in Moira's fate. Pretending to be ill in the Red Centre she tried to seduce the Angel who took her off in the ambulance, was returned in terrible pain, her feet pulled and bruised by being hit with steel cables. The Aunts and Angels like being named in a way that suggests something gentle and biblical and caring, but there is no space for free thought or free action. 'They looked like drowned feet, swollen and boneless' (102). Ironically, since in the past women cried out against big dehumanized sexual objects, now their sexual abilities for procreation are considered invaluable they are further reduced; their hands and feet are irrelevant, Aunt Lydia says, to the mission for which they are maintained, to produce babies.

This is like the worst kind of fetishized pornography in the name of the Bible and childbearing – reducing people to body parts – and this chapter emphasizes the different ways it is done, for both women and men.

Offred is constantly watched and tested.

Chapter 16

This chapter focuses on the utterly non-arousing, non-sexual act performed by the Commander in 'a regular two-four marching stroke' (105) on Offred who takes the place of Serena Joy by lying between the Wife's legs. The act has a biblical origin in the bearing of children by Bilhah, the maidservant of her barren mistress Rachel, and so is a part of the biblical referencing of the novel, and the dehumanizing experiences of being a woman in Gilead. It is sterilized, with 'underdrawers' (104) not lingerie, and a complete lack of personal interchange other than sexual, which is emphasized as dehumanizing and merely functional, since it would otherwise 'be a symptom of frivolity merely, like jazz garters or beauty spots: superfluous distractions for the light-minded . . . recreational' (105). For all this it is a serious duty, depersonalized. Offred wonders if she would prefer the Commander without his clothes but the description of his white tufted body is not attractive. After the act Serena Joy shoos her out with loathing, and so sanitized, medicalized and dehumanized is the entire exchange that as the Commander leaves, shutting the door carefully, Offred reflects that it is 'as if both of us are his ailing mother' (106). She finds it 'hilarious', but since it is deeply concerned with her own body and rights she cannot laugh.

Chapter 17

There are no cosmetics allowed in Gilead for the Handmaids, who are supposed not to care about their personal welfare or appearance since they are no more than vessels. But like the other Handmaids, Offred tries to conjure up and maintain the idea of a future life when someone will again love her 'that we will be touched again, in love or desire' (107) by hiding butter in her shoe and smearing her face with it to soften it, then feeling like she is lying as a last piece of toast for consumption. There is a strong sense of longing and loss for physical exchange, tenderness, care for others and by others in this chapter where Offred wants to be valued for herself. One way of establishing her sense of solidity as self is to steal, so she sneaks downstairs, only to encounter Nick the chauffeur. Earlier they had an exchange, forbidden but exciting, foot touching foot. Now more would be possible but utterly dangerous, so while it would be exciting, like 'shouting', 'shooting', she knows it is forbidden. Nick however has been sent to tell her the Commander would like to see her the next day in his office. Such an exchange is forbidden but has an air of being sent to the headmaster's study.

QUESTIONS

1. How does Atwood represent the ways in which minds, speech and imagination can be controlled by the regime? What alternative ways of thinking are suggested?
2. What are the various constraints and opportunities offered to men in this repressive society? How does the novel suggest the limitations of their lives?
3. There is much humour, farce, irony and satire in these chapters. How does Atwood use humour to both highlight and undercut the power of the dangers and problems of life in Gilead?

VII. Night

Chapter 18

Lying in bed in the Commander's house, Offred shifts her thoughts in time and remembers her own pregnancy in the past, lying in bed with her husband Luke, while a thunderstorm raged outside. Offred's sense of loss, lack and longing dominate

this chapter where she feels she needs the closeness of a physical, caring, relationship to feel human and whole. 'If I thought
this would never happen again I would die. But this is wrong,
nobody dies from lack of sex. It's lack of love we die from' (113).
Expressing this to her unknown audience gives her the opportunity to voice it, but there is no one who cares about her as
a person, so the final sense of her is of disembodiment, as if
confirmation of existence was dependent upon the caring and
love of another. Thinking of her past makes her think of Luke,
and Offred constructs versions of what might have happened
to him, revealing the artifice of a narrative, the ways in which
people need to develop stories to make sense to them of what
is happening. Luke could be dead, fading onto the landscape,
lying next to the dead daughter or upright in a cell, his hair cut,
his beard matted, wondering what will happen next. 'I believe
this' (114) she asserts, but in so doing undermines the validity
of the stories she constructs just to give herself some sense of
certainty, although the certainty of Luke's death is unbearable. She believes that he might be a fugitive in the resistance;
in another version he made it across the border and was saved.
Domestic and caring, she imagines him safe and 'it comforts me
to dress him warmly' (115). This indicates her needs to nurture,
but sounds like someone looking after a child or constructing
a figment of the imagination, dressing up a doll. Thinking of
gravestones, which say 'In hope' (116), Offred wonders if there
is any hope for her or for Luke. None of her beliefs are strong
enough to be real, none can be proven. 'The things I believe can't
all be true' (116) and again, 'This also is a belief of mine. This
also may be untrue' (116) undercut the certainty of anything.

VIII. Birth Day
Chapter 19
Continuing her thoughts, Offred dreams of her daughter, in a
series which both makes her vividly real, and yet leaves Offred
surrounded by images of death and loss, 'the wreath, on the
ceiling, and my curtains hanging like drowned white hair' (119).
She hoards her sanity, believing it will come in useful later.
This is a chapter about birth, past births, eggs, fertility and its
lack. There are terrifying images of past births where women

in hospital were wired up and technology helped them give
birth but also kept them prisoner, contrasted with the painful 'natural' birthing of Gilead, and there are warnings about
venereal diseases, 'Unbabies' born deformed and destroyed.
Reproductive technologies and control over women's reproduction are uppermost here.

In her reduced life, even the eating of an egg is something
Offred holds onto to remind her that she is of value. The notion
of eggs moves swiftly into her description of the day of birth for
Janine / Ofwarren's baby. This birth is also a hierarchical ceremony. The Handmaids are picked up by the Birthmobile, made
to feel they are important, and escorted out of the front door.
The Wives arrive later and are treated to comfortable seats. In
Gilead whatever kind of child is carried must be carried to term;
so important are babies that none can be terminated. However,
since there are no tests allowed on unborn babies, and since the
Gilead of the future is so polluted and suffering the effects of
a man-induced disaster, there are many problems with childbearing and the formation of babies and it is certainly the case
that some will be born with defects. Many will be deformed
and defined as Unbabies and so destroyed. The polluted world
is vividly described: 'women took medicines, pills, men sprayed
trees, cows ate grass and all that souped-up piss flowed into
the rivers. Not to mention the exploding atomic power plants
along the San Andreas fault, nobody's fault, during the earth-
quakes, and the mutant strain of syphilis no mould could touch'
(122). There was so much destruction and pollution that life
has been threatened. Offred recalls writing on ancient desks
in the schoolroom in which she and Moira once sat, which
reminded her even then of vanished civilizations, comparable
perhaps to the vanished civilization she knew before the time
of Gilead. Aunt Lydia describes the Handmaids, those who can
bear the children who will restart the future, as 'shock troops'
(122), those who go first into enemy territory and clear the way.
Rarity value is ascribed to fertile women and children but their
lives do not seem to be comfortable and the fear is that after so
much effort and pain they will merely have an Unbaby, 'give
birth to a shredder' (123). However, Aunt Lydia describes them
as pearls, valued, hard to get. The Handmaids wait for Janine
to give birth, as do the Wives, who compare the cleanliness and

usefulness of their own Handmaids. They are all joined in the event but there is no sisterhood here. Sitting up in her room, thinking of nothing, 'Ofwarren, formerly that whiny bitch Janine' (125) is the focus of attention.

Chapter 20

Staircases and chanting start this chapter, which is set in the house in which Ofwarren and her Commander and his Wife live and to which all the Handmaids and Wives are driven for the birth. It settles into a weird, hierarchical tea party with the wives supporting Warren's Wife who pretends that she, thin and grey, is giving birth while Janine struggles in a bedroom upstairs with two women 'gripping her hands, or she theirs' (127), emphasizing either control or dependency, and with a Birthing Stool and only a piece of ice to suck since all medicinal support has been denied. Aunt Lydia had emphasized that they were part of a transitional generation, and soon all thoughts of alternatives in the past would be lost as future generations of women came to accept their roles. As with earlier comments about settling into acceptance of their lot, the loss of reading and writing, the boredom; this sounds as though it offers some solace but actually is a threat. Not only does it establish the loss of freedom as normal and everyday, but the loss of any imagination or memory to try and argue that things could be otherwise. They will have less sense of alternatives, less imaginative freedom in the future. This is a worrying thought.

Remembering the options for women in the past, Offred thinks about films she was shown in the Red Centre, some informative, some pornographic, to illustrate how women were degraded and brutalized, warning the intended Handmaids about the past before the regime came to power. They also showed other films, about women who Aunt Lydia defined as wasting time. Once, when she was watching one of these films, shown without sound, – an Unwoman documentary which was meant to horrify the newly feminized women whose roles will be entirely related to their ability to procreate – she saw her mother in the days before Offred was born. Offred's mother and many others wore the kind of clothes women in the UK wore to protest at Greenham Common or on CND marches, and in the film they appear in 'Take Back the Night' marches, common in Canada. Such marches argued for the safety of the street for women walking at night, and protested about an unsafe world where women feared rape as an everyday possibility. At the same time, there were other slogans about freedom to choose, so that every baby was a wanted baby. Women were reclaiming rights over their own bodies, refusing to be victims, to be in fear of rape, or to be forced to give birth. For the Handmaids, while the rape would be a terror now removed under the regime, the idea of terminating a birth would be like blasphemy. In Gilead, freedom from violence and sexual attack has been removed, but so has any freedom for women to make choices over their own bodies. Atwood presents the contradictions and complexities of, the unexpected turns of achieving part of what these women set out to achieve.

Offred's mother seems to disappear as the balloons in the film head skywards. The glimpse is a brief snippet from the past which raises issues about freedom of choice and childbirth. Her mother's views were radical, but popular amongst second wave feminists. Men were seen as technically necessary for procreation, not unlike the way the Handmaids are seen in Gilead – a comparison which is explicit here, but not commented on by Offred. Although her mother chose to have Offred when she was 37 years old, against some outcry from her friends, her views on men are utilitarian: 'A man is just a woman's strategy for making other women' (130/1). Recalling her mother lounging, talking in her kitchen while Luke cooked, Offred portrays her as still activist, still politicized, especially after a couple of glasses of wine, and pointing out that Offred and Luke's equality was a result of the kind of pain women had suffered and the activism others engaged in. While the example of Luke slicing carrots is ironic, the argument is poignant in the circumstances, since suffering and activism underlie what they took for granted: equality in earnings and rights, equality in the kitchen.

> 'You young people don't appreciate things, she'd say. You don't know what we had to go through, just to get you where you are. Look at him, slicing up the carrots. Don't you know how many women's lives, how many women's *bodies* the tanks had to roll over just to get that far?' (131).

Excessive this may be, but Offred wants to return to that domestic simplicity and can't. 'I want her back. I want everything back, the way it was. But there is no point to it, this wanting'. (132)

Chapter 21

This chapter focuses on Janine's delivery. The performance, which is how it is described, is watched by many, as a royal birth would have been in the renaissance period. It is a difficult and painful delivery because forcibly 'natural', without drugs. Atwood emphasizes the pain and the false, sympathy pains undergone by the other Handmaids, but she also uses her characteristic humour to put it all in perspective, to see it as bizarre, and somewhat ridiculous since the skinny, older Wife is positioned straddling the birthing mother as if it were her own delivery, much as the original act of sex took place. The Wife is also awkward, out of place, performing: 'she has a tight little smile on her face, like a hostess at a party she'd rather not be giving' (135).

Atwood's wry, ironic, farcical humour appears in this difficult, painful and awkward situation as it does throughout the novel. Some of the worst activities of Gilead – hanging dissidents (such as doctors) from the Wall with hoods on their heads, or here, a very unnatural 'natural' birth – are made farcical or ironic so that the element of the absurd helps manage the full horror of the situation. In this way, Atwood offers an imaginative space, that of the comic, a distance, for the reader to cope with and deal with the horrific situation. Offred can comment on the bizarre, such as a snowman's smile on the face of a hooded, dead dissident, and she manages some of her solitary despair through black humour, focusing on the potential for suicide lying in common objects. She does not always find the scenes farcical or ironic, but there is a creative gap between her perceptions, her words and descriptions, trapped as she is in this situation and how we can distance ourselves and cope with the horror through its absurdity.

When the baby is born, the Wife is tucked up as if she had gone through labour, and is given the baby to hold, Janine's baby, which is described 'as if it's a bouquet of flowers: something she's won, a tribute' (136). Which of course it is, something to solidify her role and her marriage. But the envy of the other Wives lingers like acid on the air, like 'twittering' (136). Birdlike, dehumanized, they bear witness to the naming by the Wife (rather than by Janine, the mother who now has no other role). The child is named Angela. Janine continues to have pains, but all around her are jubilant with the triumph of a birth. However, later we find that Angela is not a survivor, is not an acceptable baby, and the connotation of her name with Angels is ironic in this respect.

The kind of sisterhood Offred's mother would have chosen is far from this collection of women supporting Janine in giving birth, although they feel false pains, breathe with her, and share her victory. 'Mother, I think. Wherever you may be. Can you hear me? You wanted a women's culture. Well, now there is one. It isn't what you meant, but it exists. Be thankful for small mercies' (137). This is part of Atwood's ironic response to some of the more blinkered, less balanced versions of feminism in the 1980s, where women's culture and society was thought to be one where there would be pure sisterhood, support, equality, no war or power struggles.

Chapter 22
Returning from the birthing in the Birthmobile Offred, exhausted, recalls the roles played in the past by both Janine, who was always collusive and did what was expected of her by the Aunts, and Moira who was always rebellious. Deviant, imaginatively energetic, Moira offers an alternative way out of the compliant behaviour enforced throughout the regime, a model of hope is seen though her extreme behaviour, although it often causes her pain in the reprisals. Janine represents complicity with power, Moira is the radical spirit. Janine, an ex-waitress, sometimes slips into a kind of trance, repeating her waitresses' patter about having a nice day and taking people's orders. She is neither very intelligent nor educated. When Offred reflects back to the time in the Rachel and Leah Centre, the Red Centre as the Handmaids called it, she compares Janine and Moira as having opposite reactions to the imposition of rules of behaviour, although Janine does occasionally burst out into something disturbed, hysterical, beyond her willingness to comply with every order and be thought well of. Janine is set up to be an informer and report on anything she hears from

the other women about Moira's escape. In a situation where people are imprisoned, their behaviour constrained and limited, a glimmer of hope, an imaginative alternative, offers the potential for escape and change and Moira represents that for Offred; it is her role in the novel.

But Offred also knows that to some extent she is constructing a story, a version of recalled events, seeing Moira as an icon of an alternative mode of behaviour, because she needs to do this. Everything reflected on, recalled, or recounted is a story, a construction. Moira escaped by taking the lever out of the toilet, capturing Aunt Elizabeth and changing clothes with her, tying her up and stowing her behind the furnace. She passed the guards by walking upright, like an Aunt would. Moira's escape resembles those prison breakouts you hear of from wartime camps, where the wit and ingenuity of the prisoners helps them tunnel out or escape in camouflage and move and speak convincingly. It offers hope, and Moira represents an alternative, keeping Offred's spirit alive. 'Moira was out there somewhere. She was at large, or dead. What would she do? The thought of what she would do expanded till it filled the room. At any moment there might be a shattering explosion, the glass of the windows would fall inwards, the doors would swing open. . . . Moira had power now, she'd been set loose, she'd set herself loose. She was now a loose woman' (143). The scenario is imaginative, idealized. Fantastic and ambiguous, because Moira, loosed on the world is also sexually free.

Chapter 23
The theme of storytelling, fictionalizing, continues as Offred acknowledges that you fictionalize when you reconstruct, reflect, re-tell events. She comments on the way in which all writing, telling, recalling shapes the truth, manages the experience. 'This is a reconstruction. All of it is a reconstruction' (144). Her hope fuels her storytelling, 'I intend to get out of here . . . when I get out of here' (144). To tell a story requires a readership however, and Offred acknowledges that some of hers might well be male and so warns them that they will never be made to feel they *should* forgive, but that forgiveness is a power too. The role of power is important here, as is the discussion of freedom throughout the novel. In all situations of

power, what matters is who has the power, who can do what to whom, and what they do with it. 'Maybe it's about who can do what to whom and be forgiven for it. Never tell me it amounts to the same thing' (145).

Offred's first unofficial meeting with the Commander has the air of a visit to the headmaster's study, as well as an aura of illegality, subterfuge, danger, ironically contrasted with the very ordinary setting and events which are made unfamiliar to Offred and us as readers. Throughout the novel, and particularly in the detail here, Atwood uses the strategies of dystopian and science fictions to defamiliarize the familiar, putting us in Offred's position and making realistic the dreadful, oppressive, limited world of Gilead. The Commander's study, filled with books which women are not allowed to read is 'an oasis of the forbidden' (147). His greeting 'Hello' is out of date and out of place so Offred feels both rather daring and also in danger, since if this lapse of formal behaviour between the Commander and her were to be discovered, he would probably receive no punishment but it would mean extradition to the colonies for her, to pick over the nuclear waste.

> 'My presence here is illegal. It's forbidden for us to be alone with the Commanders. We are for breeding purposes: we aren't concubines, geisha girls, courtesans. On the contrary: everything possible has been done to remove us from that category. There is supposed to be nothing entertaining about us, no room is to be permitted for the flowering of secret lusts; no special favours are to be wheedled, by them or us, there are to be no toeholds for love. We are two-legged wombs, that's all: sacred vessels, ambulatory chalices' (146).

This dehumanizing description clarifies the role played by the Handmaids, their ability to procreate making them seem holy and untouchable, but removing all sense of the personal, or emotional from any exchange. The discussion between the Commander and Offred proceeds with high irony. In a regime in which women are forbidden to read and write or they might seek power, the ultimate radical interaction is to play Scrabble, the word game usually chosen by children and aged relatives. The spelling of words, the holding of the counters, is described as if voluptuous, sexual. Offred's chosen words are ambiguous, also potentially sexual; 'limp', 'gorge' suggesting sexual activity; 'larynx' signifies speaking which would also be coded, limited. For Atwood, the role of Scrabble is also one which offers the opportunities of the special power of irony. It is ironic that the pomposity and terror of the regime can be undermined by the radical act of a mere word game. Atwood's comic touch offers space for Offred and readers to laugh at the ultimately potentially dangerous, even fatal interaction between the Commander and Offred, taking the Mickey, heightening the irony of the situation with the word game.

Then the Commander asks her to kiss him, which would certainly have been against the rules of relationships between them. In retelling the story of this interaction, Offred acknowledges that each version of this tale is a reconstruction, only a version. The truth is impossible to reach in recall.

QUESTIONS

1. What roles do Janine and Moira play in the novel and to what effect?
2. How does Atwood use elements of comedy to help manage the terrible oppressive world of Gilead and Offred's experiences within it?
3. What issues about women's bodies, birth and rights are explored in these chapters?

IX. Night

Chapter 24

The theme of storytelling continues. Offred discusses what are usually seen as realistic ways of putting things into perspective, also seen as arranging them, as 'the illusion of depth, created by a frame' (153). We wonder how to actually trust Offred's tale as any kind of a record as she too is concerned about what is real. This late into the novel, she starts to give us the kind of realistic details of herself which one would find in conventional narrative: that she is 33, five foot seven with brown hair. She raises the issue of the interpretation of events and what can be considered true, what false, what constructed, and how the speaker and the receiver of any version of an event interpret and construct differently in relation to their context. In this respect, much of what we might believe and pass on, could be a fiction we are constructing for ourselves. The nature of truth, reality, sense making and storytelling are important here and so are issues of guilt, honesty and the duty to take note of any possible culpability in events. 'Context is all' (154) offers an explanation of different perspectives, even of what could be considered factual, but the example of the concentration camp supervisor's mistress which follows suggests the culpability of refusing to face up to realities.

Offred remembers a woman in a TV programme who lived an elegant life with a swimming pool and nice clothes, while next door, in the concentration camp run by her lover, Jews were gassed and murdered. 'The woman said she didn't notice much that she found unusual. She denied knowing about the ovens' (155). The woman, interviewed, said that she did not feel that this man, her lover, was a monster. She got used to his behaviour, and their surroundings, as normal, everyday. However, her own performativity, her performing of a certain role, refusing to face the unpalatable truths, was emphasized in the vast amounts of make-up she wore during those years and also later when she is interviewed. This emphasizes that her response to the public and to herself is a cover up, an artifice, self-delusion. After the filming of the interview her recollection must have been something that opened up her conscience and self-awareness of what had really happened, how she had colluded through ignoring what was going on, overlooking the part she played in the brutal regime under Nazism. Recognizing the truth, she killed herself.

We switch to Offred who feels something is cracking. She dissolves in desperate hysterical laughter. Rocking, broken, she passes out on the floor, to be discovered the next day by Cora bringing in her breakfast eggs. Facing up to events can be too unbearable.

X. Soul Scrolls

Chapter 25

In a context where procreation, fecundity and fertility are all, the breaking of an egg (Offred's breakfast) is like a small death. When Cora finds Offred on the floor she is worried that there has been a second suicide. Meanwhile in the garden we see Serena Joy cutting off the seed pods from the flowers and Offred carrying a basket of lamb chops. This spring time of fruitfulness is one of painful non-productivity for women, particularly Offred who notes that 'spring has now been undergone' (160) as if it were a trial. Summer dresses, willow trees, light, heat and flowers are all filled with, redolent with the sense of fertility, productivity, ripeness, in contrast to Offred's own lack of pregnancy. It is also in contrast with the decreed activities of the Wives, who produce knitted garments instead of children, and seek bed rest for minor illnesses or invented ailments while other more ordinary woman dare not be ill for fear of being banished as useless since 'You don't see that many old women around any more' (162). The economics of gender and power mean that only fertile women are worth anything. The others, the infertile and old women, are worthless and sent to the colonies.

This chapter also deals with the developing relationship with the Commander who now offers Offred an illicit illegal old copy of *Vogue* to entertain her. The magazine promised impartiality and 'dealt in transformations' (165), showing poised, powerful, self-aware, and performative, posturing women in the days when they both dressed up and indicated that they could make their own decisions and actions. Relics of a bygone era, magazines which Offred would have discarded in a few moments previously because they are empty, filled with artificial promise, are now at a premium, since the magazines are supposed to have all been destroyed. This is another indication of the power of the Commander, that he can hide, and share the illicit magazine with Offred. The difference in their positions emerges as he shows genuine lack of understanding about what is missing from her life and what she asks for now. They are now more in a covert relationship but she also lets him know that razor blades with which she could kill herself, along with books and writing materials are all absent from her life. Lack and threat define her, and to him, she feels she is a captive strange creature. He is 'looking in through the bars' and she is 'only a whim' (168). These words emphasize their different positions of power. Offred's lack of empowerment is in contrast with the

Commander's easy ownership of what is allowed, what is illicit but controlled. These items and freedoms are available to him, indications of power for him; rules are there to be broken. The comic, ironic element is the banality of their relationship: 'so there it was, out in the open: his wife didn't understand him' (166). This is a cliché of relationships between married men and their mistresses, of which that between Offred and the Commander is a parody since he has all the power, and there is no sexual interaction.

Chapter 26

We hear about the actual 'Ceremony' again in this chapter. That Offred and the Commander have some kind of illicit relationship, however, makes the Ceremony of sexual interaction, intercourse, embarrassing, more intimate, less depersonalized and this is dangerous for Offred. She has to warn the Commander about any change in his behaviour, while she herself starts to notice other awkward things about her own body, such as her hairy legs. In a normal relationship she would have had the power and expectation to change her appearance, should she decide to, but here she is 'uncouth' involved not in love making but an 'act of copulation, fertilization' (170). Because of their interactions in the study, the Ceremony now feels like 'filching' the husband from the Wife. Offred feels a little shamefaced about it in this bizarre situation. Aunt Lydia's version of a future sisterhood in which there would be no jealousies, is idealistic and a parody of the feminist idealism of the 1980s.

There are confused feelings in the triangular relationship now established between Serena Joy, Offred and the Commander. 'For the generations that come after, Aunt Lydia said, it will be so much better. The women will live in harmony together' (171). Her view is that it will amount to the sharing of chores and the managing of different roles so that women will no longer be burdened with all the female roles – wife, mistress, mother, cleaner and so on – at once. This ideal, Aunt Lydia's view, is a warped version of feminist analysis, identifying that women were forced to undertake too many roles, to be superwomen. We can see that Aunt Lydia's version now would be and indeed is divisive, hardly likely to lead to sisterly support. The only

positive for Offred is that she means something; she is in some
kind of a role, not merely an empty vessel.

Chapter 27

The chapter starts out as a shopping trip but develops important connections between the two Handmaids, Offred and
Ofglen, since it is now that they both realize neither is pious and
compliant and each would like to live differently with more freedom. Though they have been shopping and walking together
for months it takes a long time to trust anyone as there are so
many spies and so much playing of games, conforming with the
regime. There are explicit comparisons with the days of consumption and choice, not least since it is these same streets that
used to be shopping streets and which now only provide the
basics, when they are available. As Offred walks along to the
shops, she remembers ice cream parlours and clothes in the past
and tells us that, in order to emphasize the illegality of women
reading, the shops are given simple biblical names – Loaves and
Fishes, Daily Bread and signs are put in the windows if there
is produce to buy, although there are many shortages and poor
quality food. Their freedom to change their walking route is
part of the book's debate about the nature of freedom. In fact
there is so little freedom for them that even a minor decision
about the route feels eventful and Offred compares them to rats,
scientific subjects and victims. 'A rat in a maze is free to go any-
where, as long as it stays inside the maze' (174). Piety is clearly
both necessary and a sham. The Wives, we're told, pay for many
prayers to be muttered on the mechanical scroll produced on a
machine, amusingly called 'Holy Roller', at 'Soul Scrolls', a religious store which prints out prayers and talks through them.
Offred remembers that it used to be a lingerie store instead –
clearly something far too frivolous for the republic. However,
since the prayers are bought over the phone and muttered
behind shatterproof glass, piety is a pretence. In this way the
Wives indicate their religious conformism but the expense and
the noting of their purchase of prayers is enough – they don't
need to do anything with the aim, intent, or meaning of the
prayers which are quietly muttered in the shop. Spirituality has
become a total sham in this regime where the letter of the Bible
is constantly used (rather than the spirit of it) to control and

force conformity. Re-naming the mechanical system at Soul Scrolls as 'Holy Rollers' is amusing, cartoon like, at odds with this control. Mentioning the Tibetan prayer wheels reminds us of the Chinese control of Tibet to Nepal, another religious and political regime. Hope rises in Offred. However, the next event is the mugging of a seemingly insignificant pedestrian by the police, who trawl the streets like sharks in their vans. The man is attacked and bundled into the dark van. In such a destructive situation, Offred's only relief is that it wasn't her they picked on. Against this surveillance and tyranny stands Offred's hope that there could be an underground, a radical movement which could offer a way out, an alternative. Its existence is revealed by Ofglen, surreptitiously and in a coded manner. Atwood's style also offers a way of managing the oppression. Her use of humour in the naming of shops, the scrolls, and her placing of the prison and turrets in the inner sanctum of Harvard, with its library, are all ironic. In the centre of learning (of today and the 1980s) lies what will become, in the near future, the centre of manipulation, control, lies and destruction. Women are not allowed in the ex-university now, except to attend the Women's Salvagings where, we later discover, they are punished for sins such as adultery or abortion, all related to their taking control over their own bodies.

Chapter 28

In many ways this chapter is the core of the novel. It focuses on the exact moment in Offred's history, and that of Gilead, when the old way of life fell, was broken up and destroyed, and the new regime established by force. It is a record of a political coup conducted by armed troops from an army other than the regular army, and so more frightening, less related to accountable power. Importantly, for a novel which concentrates on the dystopian future for women, it is a terrifying warning about how easy it could be to disempower women, remove equality and revert to a situation even less just in terms of equal rights than that of the Victorian era. Offred starts this chapter remembering Moira, whose feelings about men and their power have fed into her realization that she prefers women as partners. Moira represents the energies of non conformism, individualism and refusal. In the past they are talking, then

Offred cuts to the apartment with Luke and her daughter, a normal everyday relationship in an ordinary place. Later, what she both details and familiarizes is the normality of her life as a woman who has a job, her own bank account, freedom and equality, a lifestyle women in the past were used to. Suggesting historical distance, difference, she reminds herself of the archaic use of paper money, referred to as 'those pieces of paper' (182). And then she tells us about the terrible day after 'the catastrophe' which remains indescribable. Apparently Islamic fanatics attacked and machine-gunned the Congress, but the details are inexact, and who is to blame is always too vague to pin down. Congress was shot, the Constitution suspended, martial law enforced, but with an army which was not familiar, as if secret forces had already been there ready in the wings waiting for such a terrible event. Moira is not surprised and she is less surprised later when Offred meets direct, swift, silent, removal of her rights. Offred's story resembles a piece of testimony from a survivor, like the series of testimonies about 9/11 which followed its embedding in the memory and psyche of the West. Going about her daily business with normality, she drops her child off at day care on an ordinary morning and visits the corner shop to buy cigarettes. Her behaviour is regular, everyday, but the scene is defamiliarized and suddenly threatening, absent, empty, confusing. In a situation where no paper money exists, everyone has ended up using Compucards to access their money, much as we use debit and credit cards today. Their numbers are checked into whatever outlet they are buying from and their accounts debited. But not this morning. Instead of the usual woman in the corner shop there is a strange man who doesn't know how to operate the system. He declares that Offred's card is not valid. This is irritating, but not yet dreadful, though as readers with hindsight we realize that it is the first stage in the total removal of women's identity or subjectivity. 'He knew some private joke he wasn't going to tell me' (185) hints at the undercurrent of a hidden story which begins to emerge later in the day when the director of their work area enters their library workspace. They are putting all hard copies of books onto discs, destroying the originals, much as paper money was destroyed. Clearly distressed the director says that they all have to go, they must be let go. In the hallways armed guards wait to break things, to act with force, to get rid of the women. Offred and the others, stunned, realize that all their powers, rights and freedoms are removed at a single swipe. The cards and bank accounts are frozen, their equal status wiped out. 'F's are no longer equivalent to 'M's and there is nothing that can be done. It is all centralized, mechanized, imposed and final. The utter lack of individual rights is terrible. The disempowerment, the vacuum, the lack of energy is tangible. Offred has nothing to do, nowhere to go and no one to talk to at home. She hugs the cat to give herself a sense of reality, she stares from her window, her life is reduced to a powerless vacuum, the regime has removed her identity and her power as a woman, just because she is a woman. This is a terrible scenario, feared by feminists as a kind of excessive parody of a return to the Victorian age when women could not own property, had no value except for their relationship to male relatives and had no rights. From a twentieth and twenty-first century perspective, such 'ancient' history is a terrible threat to us today, but it is close, possible, notes Offred. Her mother warned her of its possibility. With hindsight she realizes that they lived in a kind of false security. Moira was not surprised by events. It is as if the qualities of the previous years had all been a sham, and de-energized, disempowered, she has nothing to do, she is depressed. Women cannot own property, so Luke will gain access to her money. In this situation, in a caring relationship or an economic relationship, this should mean that women can access their own money, by proxy, although it will only diminish rather than grow since they have no jobs any more. Moira and her friends have sorted out an alternative solution, intending to identify gay men who can access their accounts. Kindliness is uppermost, a form of paternalism, since men have the power it is in their power to enable women to have their own money and limited rights. Offred nonetheless feels a tangible shift of power when Luke says 'I'll always take care of you' (188). He means it kindly of course, and he did not initiate either the regime or the situation, but Offred's position is powerless, consequently she feels this is patronizing and her own response is paranoid. A feminist informed differentiation is helpful here. 'Patriarchy' means oppressive male control, 'paternalism' is at least intended to be fatherly and caring (both come from the same root word – pater, father) and 'patronizing' in this context would seem to mean emphasizing one's power over another, undermining and undercutting their power, letting them know you are in control. It is alarming to Offred to recognize that her hatred of paternalism is uppermost. This can seem paranoid but the context is important here. If all women's power is removed and placed under the powerful control of others who happen to be male then a knock on effect is that values, rights and economics are so shifted that women are treated as worthless. This would necessarily seem monstrous, the response paranoid but real. And what is doubly terrifying is that there is no one to react against, no one to complain to. The silent, absent, unelected control force takes no prisoners and puts up with no complaints. Marches are dangerous, fatal. This is total power. In this situation the feminist focus shifts also into one of political awareness of the difficult and dangerous situation which everyone is placed under in a totalitarian regime. The balance of power and agency have changed in Offred's relationship with Luke. 'We are not each other's, any more. Instead, I am his' (191). But she realizes she needs to comply since she cannot afford to lose him – literally.

Chapter 29

This chapter focuses entirely on one of Offred's visits to the Commander's office, which seems rather like 'a bank customer negotiating a hefty loan' (193) where, although relaxed in her long red dress and her legs tucked up, she is in a changing relationship with him. They play Scrabble, he is paternalistic or 'daddyish' and because reading is an illicit activity for women when she reads he takes a licentious, almost sexual pleasure in watching her. He has allowed her magazines and now literature but in this visit they talk and we discover that he first worked in market research, then as a kind of scientist. Offred checks the phrase 'nolite te bastardes carborundum' with him – the one scrawled on the cupboard wall in her room by the previous Handmaid. When he reveals that this is schoolboy Latin and shows her more examples she realizes that the previous Handmaid was also allowed into his private realm and read some of his books, prior to hanging herself. Aunt Lydia's use of a phrase 'Pen Is Envy' (penis envy: a Freudian term for women who wish for male power, one pointed out and critiqued by feminist theorists). She plays on words and by so doing reveals the relationship between power, language and sexuality, where language as a form of communication and expression enables and lack of it disables. She has some room for manoeuvre as they collude in this relationship.

This chapter provides insights into power games, the control of people's lives by language, access to language, and privilege. In this economy of gendered power, Offred has only her role as a potential child producer with which to negotiate, but the new relationship with the Commander both casts her into more sexual interaction with him and emphasizes how, even under the strictest regimes, those with power can bend the rules. For the Commander, word games, flirting, and the offering of insights into language, writing, knowledge are all possible ways in which he can exercise his power.

QUESTIONS

1. How does Offred's relationship with the Commander change? What are the signs and what does this say about their different positions of power?
2. How does Atwood bring the coup to life? What modes of writing does she use to make it both immediate and terrifying?
3. How are strategies of the comic used in these chapters and to what ends?

XI. Night

Chapter 30

This is a chapter about longing and restraint, loss and despair. In the novel we are following the personal responses of an individual and here Offred runs through many versions of denial and lack. It is sensitive, emotionally painful and really realistic, not a chapter of philosophical debate but one which makes us aware of how Offred feels. Seeing Nick the chauffeur she has a sense of a potential relationship in contrast to the romantic ones of Shakespeare's time with lutes, roses, balcony scenes, only leaving regulations, and hunger, a real need for love and comfort, sex, closeness – all of which are not allowed.

The description of the night sky in a post nuclear landscape is powerful. Like the alteration of word meanings such as shop titles, Prayvaganzas leading to mass weddings, Particicutions mean butcherings, Salvagings are political murders, each of the indications of a beautiful night sky is undercut by its nuclear waste context, while night flowers bloom and remind her of her physicality; the red on the horizon is not sunset but 'red radiation, wavering upwards like the shimmer above highway tarmac at noon' (201). Hard words – radiation, tarmac – contrast with the exciting beauty of the sunset. And unable to indulge in beauty, romance, she knows that the Commander's critique of women's ability to add (a commonplace, stereotypical image) that is, that they cannot make 'one and one and one and one' (201) add to four but leave it as the separated single numbers, leads her to celebrate this as an advantage. Instead of showing a lack, an inability, it shows perception of individuality. Offred agrees – since each is individualized, not part of a homogeneity and statistical analysis. 'Each one remains unique' (201), so Atwood turns the language of criticism into that of recognition of individuals, of celebration; clever wordplay.

Then Atwood give us a phrase altered from *King Lear*, Shakespeare's play, in which Lear, betrayed by his own delusions about the care of his calculating daughters, realizes all one can do in life is reach one's full potential – though here Offred alters it; 'context is all, or is it ripeness?' (202) (in *Lear* it is ripeness). She stretches her arms out to memories of Luke and her daughter and the cat and can't hang onto the images anymore; while she prays it's in reality about survival as she goes through the standard words of prayer, analysing their meaning for her own context, since language has its meaning only in context. There is a theme cutting across this lack and longing and it is that of death, pointless death and betrayal. She remembers how they had to prepare to slip away, just prior to being betrayed by neighbours and so being caught. Offred remembers too, how they realized they had to kill their cat not to give themselves away and how in these circumstances, there is a move away from naming individuals – in this case the cat – to labelling what you must destroy as 'it'. In a similar way, scientists label dogs, chinchillas and rats, not as themselves but 'the dog model' when about to experiment on them in order to remove compassion. This and the statistical numbering contribute to a debate about the importance of the individual, set against the dehumanization of the state. Offred's messages are all and only to God since she has no idea who else might hear her, no idea of an audience. Themes of communication and power emerge here, as language is slippery and changed, and yet tied to values.

XII. Jezebel's
Chapter 31
The previous chapter left Offred wondering how she could continue to live and this chapter starts in much the same vein, emphasizing loss which readers can immediately recognize, a desire to turn the clock back to how things used to be. It's quite emotionally wrenching. 'Every night when I go to bed I think, In the morning I will wake up in my own house and things will be back the way they were. It hasn't happened this morning, either' (209).

The chapter is fragmented as Offred wonders about losing engagement with 'greyout', loss, and managing somehow, steering a course between sentimentality about what is lost, such as eggs, and being so inured to it that she can cope. While previously she contemplated suicide by hanging from the chandelier, now she is sitting in her chair in the heat waiting for the day to just turn round. These chapters focus on the ways in which people genuinely try to deal with the unmanageable, with loss, pain and situations of extreme threat or deprivation. Too much engagement, too much pain at loss destroys them; too much silent coping takes away the will to live. She and Ofglen think about how Jewish people, 'Sons of Jacob' (210) managed to get out of Gilead and they have to undergo a ritual viewing of those hanging on the Wall, one a catholic, one labelled 'J', but not a Jew. Their talk is limited, described as 'amputated speech' (211), truncated, clipped to remain safe, the limitation of expression makes her opportunity for communication with her audience, us, more poignant and valuable and reminds us of how many people under fundamentalist or other repressive regimes cannot ever have their voices heard because the outlets are too dangerous, they have no way of writing, no way of getting the experiences out to others; power denies them their expression. This chapter then, as the previous one, considers the ability and daring to speak and the importance of audience in moments of censorship and silence, on hearing of the individual experience. What does emerge is the exchange of a password, 'Mayday', which Offred is told stands for the French 'help me, m'aidez' – and is an underground language. The 'network' Ofglen speaks of has an extended and subtly more important meaning now than the 'networking' practised by her old friends – where networking meant having lunch. In times of constraint and loss, some of the behaviours taken for granted are of real worth.

Returning to the house, Offred is brought into a dangerous collusion with Serena Joy who has her own agenda, setting Offred up with Nick the chauffeur. She is mindful of the fact that Offred's time is running out, as Serena Joy puts it, so 'someone we trust' (215) could help out. This plot to service Offred so that there could be a child is an indication of Serena Joy's own agenda not sisterhood, however it seems, and it is both a way of satisfying some of Offred's longing for human interaction and immensely dangerous; for the previous Handmaid, who in all likelihood also participated in illicit Scrabble games with the Commander, such collusion ended in hanging. In order to persuade her, Serena Joy offers her first a photo of her daughter, which would prove she was alive, and then a cigarette. This shows her power and releases Offred into another space but is immensely dangerous, as are the activities with the Commander in the next few chapters.

Chapter 32

This is a chapter which starts with possible women bonding as Offred talks with Rita round the kitchen table and asserts her new found status. But in asking for a match, one element of her sense of power, as ever, is about deviant behaviours. This deviant behaviour is not about stealing but potentially burning the house down. Meanwhile, with the Commander, the relationship has developed into one where he introduces a tinge of dissipation as he drinks and likes to play subservient to the woman, who has absolutely no power. He leads into a discussion of how men had become unable to relate to or have a role with women under the old modes of behaviour. He argues that with women's power and equality men were, as a result, turning off sex, marriage, everything, as if the argument were that relationships could only continue if there were inequalities of power. The regime, he admits, intended to be better, but in a brief window into the problems of political change he notes, 'Better never means better for everyone' (222). This chapter reveals issues to do with power, balance, gender interactions and the problems of attempting change, either to revert to a previous set relationship or to establish something new. As such it moves beyond the context of Gilead and causes readers to think about varieties of power relationships.

Chapter 33

The Handmaids are off to a Prayvaganza which sounds like some festival but in fact is a staged mass marriage event which is ostensibly religious with girls as young as fourteen, dressed as sacrificial virgins in white, married off to Angels (troops) without any mutual love. The scene of the Handmaids walking two by two as if they are girls from a private school or in a fairy tale is matched by the stony-faced young men at the doorway, 'plaster-hard young faces' (225) which emphasises the artifice and game playing. The setting for the Prayvaganza, mass wedding, is, like many others in Gilead, in ironic contrast to the activity itself. This rather sacrificial mass wedding is very like a school sports day with wooden chairs in rows for the Wives and a cordoned off area for the Handmaids, who are not merely spectators but are expected to act.

Control over their bodies is emphasized in the discussion between Ofglen and Offred in which they discuss Janine's baby, born a few chapters earlier. Named Angela too soon, reminding us of the word angel, the baby was 'shredded' (226). Marriages and procreation might dominate Gilead but the infertility and birth defects are overwhelming. The women of Gilead are in the service of the attempt to create a new generation, but the generation to which they all belong is guilty of polluting the water, the land, the air, and now of controlling lives. There are so many man-made mistakes which have resulted in disastrous consequences, emphasized in the quality of life in Gilead, that this novel is rightly seen as making an early powerful ecological statement about sustainability, and its opposite, pollution, dev-astation, annihilation. Later work by Atwood, including both *Oryx and Crake* (2003) and *The Year of the Flood* (2009), con-tinues this theme.

Breakdown in the face of terrible pressure and dehumaniza-tion has appeared already in the novel in Offred's contemplation of suicide with thoughts of secreting a cord to hang herself from a nonexistent chandelier, or taking a knife from the kitchen to cut her wrists. Janine earlier broke down and started acting out her job as a waitress, as if in an obsessive routine, until the young women at Aunt Lydia's Red Centre snapped her out of it. The novel asks the reader questions about the results of totalitarian regimes. It asks questions about the performance of roles, how to gain some meaning in your life, and the relation of power and individual self-worth.

Chapter 34

This chapter focuses on women's roles, marriage prospects past and present, and different view about sex and its enjoyment. The Prayvaganza or mass wedding takes place. Silent girls in white are married off, unseen, to Angels, young men newly returned from the battle front. Later in the evening, the Commander talks of what women have gained in the new regime. This relates to the themes of feminism and women's lives. Previously at the 'meat market', personal ads indicated that many women were desperate to find partners but could not, while others had their pick. Marriage was followed by abuse, violence, husbands walking out, not taking their responsibilities seriously and some mothers bringing up their children on too little money – with money as the only measure, women had 'no respect as mothers. No wonder they were giving up on the whole business. This way they're protected, they can fulfil their biological destinies in peace. With full support and encouragement' (231). The argu-ment derives from paternalism, where women are considered in need of protection. Paternalism is more 'daddyish' (as Offred defines the Commander in this mood) and seemingly kindly since it has women's interests at heart, but the attitude taken towards women, one of protection, assumes that they are sec-ondary citizens, dependant, helpless without the abilities and opportunities afforded men, and in this scenario only defined by their biological destinies, seen entirely as childrearing. If that were all women were for, then a rigid protected scenario might well be suitable, but women had been recognized as human equals and to have equal rights, at least in developed countries. Since the second half of the nineteenth century and first half of the twentieth century, equal rights means more to life than protection for breeding purposes, another way of defining what the Commander describes here. Offred points out what is missing from this depiction of human relations as entirely for procreation for the republic – 'Love' (231). Both he and Aunt Lydia scorn the idea of romantic love, falling in love, defining it as a fluke, leading to more problems than arranged marriages. In many other societies this argument is made fluently and so the issue of romantic love with all its individualistic mistakes, and arranged marriages with their intention of producing children, are perspectives and practices which are set against each other. Offred's support for romantic love derives not just from her own experiences, but her investment in the importance of individual choice rather than enforced regulation, and so is part of her need to maintain a hold on her own freedom of expression, even though this is only through the verbal testimony and free thoughts still somewhat regulated through the conditions imposed on naming and language as well as free speech and exchange with others.

The ceremony of marriage at the Prayvaganza which follows is reminiscent of a rather warped manipulation of biblical language and nineteenth century male propaganda perpetrated by such as John Ruskin in *Of Queens' Gardens* (1865) and in the medical journals such as *The Lancet* at that time; propaganda which insisted that women should not be allowed to study and teach (in the medical journals this was backed up by arguments that to do so would lead to atrophy of childbearing abilities). Offred has sympathy for the girls – they are stuck with whoever they are now paired with, zits and all. The memory of Aunt Lydia suggesting women could develop camaraderie dissolves into Moira's hints of Aunt Lydia's potential for the sexual exploitation of Janine. This set of radical naughty thoughts provides Offred with an escape valve in the context of the ritual weddings. Her own relationship of sorts with the Commander is then acknowledged by Ofglen who asks that if she hears anything at all about anything to pass it on. This chapter focuses on deviancy and freedom, in the context of constraint.

Chapter 35

This chapter continues the exploration of constraint, love and whether it is worth expending the energy to fight back against a controlling regime. Offred's play on words here explores issues of falling, falling in love, being a fallen woman, falling, free floating as a pleasant and dangerous experience which characterizes the freedoms and securities yet allied insecurities. In a version of domestic horror, questioning love and relationships, the loved one appears familiar and safe and then sometimes as a complete stranger, revealed in the moonlight, acting out of character. This reminds her of a serial killer, mutilations, bodies chopped up and left in freezers. The oscillation between caring security and the unknown are all involved in male female relationships, and freedom from some of the worst experiences of violent abuse seems to be a product of life in the republic. Offred considers the obsessional quality of being almost addicted to someone else's body and presence, explored here with an honesty and a kind of detached scrutiny only possible when the relationships themselves are being reflected on, as Offred's is, at a distance. It provides a fascinating scrutiny and exploration of varieties of possible interactions, issues of honesty, compulsion, obsession, loss. Around this there also exists a sometimes dangerous insecurity. The freedom to make choices and change emerges as one lost but held valuable. 'It's strange to remember how we used to think, as if everything were available to us, as if there were no contingencies, no boundaries; as if we were free to shape and reshape forever the ever-expanding perimeters of our lives. I was like that too, I did that too' (239). But it is irrevocably past and clearer because a memory, and now a sad loss. 'I'm a refugee from the past' (239) Offred declares, so she revisits, like a stranger, the quaint scenarios of her own history. This chapter emphasizes the loss of items we take for granted as Offred once did, the freedom to choose and the lack of any awareness that this could change. When Cora, who usually brings her tray for supper, is replaced by Serena Joy with the photograph of Offred's lost daughter, the emphasis on what memories contain, what is constant, what solid, what ephemeral is brought home to her. Here there are comments on ways in which we make sense of our own history through reflection, and the insubstantiality of memories and reflection. Despite their insubstantiality, memories and reflection offer necessary traces to reassure about the value of life, of individuality and choice, emphasized in the energies of this chapter and those around it. While the public arguments are made for control, safety, resignation, rituals and arranged marriage, paternalism and regulation, nonetheless, the memories, energies and awareness of falsifying events through wordplay emphasize and undercut the blinkered, intolerant insistence on certain perceptions and ways of life. Critique is uppermost, enabled through wordplay, a form of freedom used by both Atwood, and Offred. In these chapters the debate about free thinking and free choice, individualism and romantic love, identity and language, memory and relationships in a free world are validated by Offred's personal evaluations and dialogue between the past and the present. Seeing that her daughter has grown up, she is both thankful for her safety and yet feels 'erased' (240) from her life. The final moment shows her eating alone commenting on the lack of a knife. Several chapters, however upbeat in reinforcing the values of the remembered past and the life spirit in the context of the restrained and wretched present, nonetheless end with the possibility of suicide, from which Offred just pulls back and moves on, into the next chapter.

Chapter 36

Where there is power there is the opportunity for those in power to bypass their own rules. Since the power in Gilead focuses on curtailing freedoms of belief, politics and individual choice, in particular in relation to procreation and sexual relationships, it is perhaps not surprising that the Commander can abuse the power which restrains others' sexual freedoms. We are told he is very high up in the power structure, and so he should be able to smuggle Offred into a licensed but highly selective brothel/nightclub, disguised as a 'night out'. She must pretend to be several women in order to take part it in the 'little' moment of freedom he has in mind, his personal way of flaunting his power, breaking the rules about entertainment, and the strict rules about use of women. Offred notes that he uses the word 'little' several times, diminishing the danger, acting playful, diminishing her. She must act several roles, first as a Wife to get through security guards along the route, then as a totally non person hiding on the floor of the car, and finally as an evening rental. Offred realizes, as she puts on the outdated, tatty, over tight, ridiculously ostentatious, skimpy dress of a nightclub performer, perhaps someone from a cabaret, that she is not the first person he has smuggled in to this brothel/club. He obviously took previous Handmaids, including the one who hanged herself, Offred's predecessor. Commander Fred enjoys his power and the breaking of rules. This emphasizes the hypocrisy of such regimes or any controlling force which cannot see its own contradictions or monitor its own obedience to rules which are forced on those who have less power, usually for economic reasons, their poverty, or because they are not forceful, political, well connected. Abuse of power undercuts the high handed moral tone of the republic. Along with the comic, the absurd, and wordplay, Atwood's exposure of such contradictions is another of her ways to satirize both what is happening in Gilead, and also other regimes and structures where controlling beliefs leave no space for criticism, irony or difference. The tone of the relationship between Offred and the Commander has also become a mixture of playful, keeping the dangerous and illicit at arm's length, while she is aware at every moment that should she be caught, playing Scrabble in his study, wearing spangles and feathers in a brothel, she would be the one punished. His boyish control over her pleasure – a magazine, a night out, hand cream, emphasizes the inequalities of power deriving from their gender roles in this society. Giving her the faded, glittery, spangled dress, he plays 'animal, vegetable, or mineral' a child's game in which she has to guess what the object more nearly resembles. He defines it as animal. It is in effect a dressing up costume, 'glittering and theatrical' (242), 'an old theatre costume'. This is ironic since, in the past, most of these were burned with glee by second wave feminists such as her mother. Articles of clothing which turned women into sexual objects were burned in separate bonfires from the bonfire of pornographic books and magazines which depicted women in humiliating ways, as sexual objects. These burnings were a mainstream, celebrated act: 'In New York it was called the Manhattan Cleanup. There were bonfires in Times Square, crowds chanting around them, women throwing their arms up thankfully into the air when they felt the cameras on them, clean-cut stony-faced young men tossing things onto the flames, armfuls of silk and nylon and fake fur, lime-green, red, violet; black satin, gold lame, glittering silver; bikini underpants, see-through brassieres with pink satin hearts sewn on to cover the nipples' (242). In this detailed, realistic mixture of brightly coloured underclothes being thrown away and burned there are both the clothes worn by glamour models or found in sex shops, those which feminists might feel demean women, and colourful things which women might choose to wear because they felt good and made them feel good. In throwing away the pornography and the sexually licentious and demeaning, everything went indiscriminately on the pile, the pyre. Feminism's desire to prevent women being seen as sex objects was therefore oddly collusive with a growing, male controlled regime – the stony-faced young men – which later developed beyond the imagination of the joyous feminists, into a repression and prevention of any kind of individualism or of any kind of control over the body. In such a scene, Atwood shows how extremes develop, how changes of behaviour and control, powerful decisions can seep into society without people seeing their implications.

The Commander uses 'an archaic phrase' (243) when he says he's 'taking' Offred 'out', since she never goes out for enjoyment or entertainment. This trip, however, is both about showing off and dressing up, and about hiding, lying. She is going out, undercover. Offred wears Serena Joy's cloak to pretend to be his Wife. She uses a fake pass as a Wife, and hides under the car seat when going past a checkpoint through which no women would be allowed. Then, when they reach the back door of the hotel which is now Jezebel's (after the immoral biblical prophetess in Revelations, New Testament) she turns into an 'evening rental' with a tag, like 'airport luggage', (245) on the wrist to show ownership and power. The Commander's orders to Nick emphasize that he and Offred are both 'functionaries', they just have parts to play in the Commander's game. His reminder to Nick about when to pick them up informs Offred that this has happened before, she is not the first. She wonders if Nick finds the whole scenario distasteful; although they have no real relationship as yet, she seeks his approval. In Offred's head, Moira makes a comment. Moira is always the internal radical voice of clarity about her behaviour, a measure against which to check her responses about power, female behaviour, individuality: 'Idiot, says Moira' (245).

Chapter 37

The next chapter takes place in Jezebel's, which Offred realizes, ironically, is the same hotel in which she used to meet Luke in the afternoons, before they were married. This makes the whole event particularly poignant and absurd. All the hotel's corridors, rooms and furnishings have been adapted to make it appropriate for a high class, illicit, politically approved brothel/ club where those in power can meet and have fun with the women who are kept there. 'It was a hotel, then. Now it's full of women' (246) emphasizes the change in role. Also, ironically, the sisterliness of the place becomes evident later on, when Offred spends time in the ladies room, after she has recognized Moira, exchanged secret signs and found a reason to momentarily escape. The scene is excessive, the men are all in black and look like politicians or business men, all alike. The women are over dressed in outfits from various periods. They wear kinds of costumes which emphasize different versions of women from different times, places, contexts. So they wear a variety of clothing ranging from baby doll pyjamas to cabaret costume and sports clothes. In the twenty-first century, one might think of the stereotypical representations of girl bands, such as the Spice Girls, who each represented a type from the sporty to the sophisticated and elegant. In this range of fanciful versions of women, Atwood details the different outfits. The women are multicoloured, exotic, 'tropical' (246) in 'outfits', 'costumes'(247) dressed for an event, a performance, and all heavily made up, emphasizing both the sexuality and the clownishness of make-up, the promise, performance and artifice.

> 'All wear make-up, and I realize how unaccustomed I've become to seeing it, on women, because their eyes look too big to me, too dark and shimmering, their mouths too red, too wet, blood-dipped and glistening; or, on the other hand, too clownish.

At first glance there's a cheerfulness to this scene. It's like a masquerade party; they are like oversized children, dressed up in togs they've rummaged from trunks. Is there joy in this? There could be, but have they chosen it? You can't tell by looking.

There are a great many buttocks in this room. I am no longer used to them.' (247)

It is a masquerade; they are like children – all of which suggests the performativity of women, on show for men's pleasure, amusingly rounded off with the comment about buttocks. Offred is unused to seeing either flesh or make-up. Women in Gilead have strict roles, and wear the colour coded costumes which indicate such roles – green for Marthas who do the household chores, blue for wives, red for handmaids. They also never wear clothes which emphasize their sexuality. The Commander enjoys the scene because 'it's like walking into the past' (247) and of course it is, so re-entering gives him a sense of power. But it is a past in which women performed roles, dressed up, were recognized only for their sexual and ornamental performance, in contrast to the hierarchical and feigned roles of the Gilead republic. Offred's own experience is contradictory. She feels oddly both out of place and in familiar surroundings, shorn of her white Handmaid's wings so lighter, but overwhelmed by the dressing up. Once she meets up with Moira she finds the conversation with her and her friends liberating. This contradictory set of responses emphasizes the contrasting conditions for women – before the Republic of Gilead and during it – in which neither situation or condition would be ideal, both problematic for women. Offred recognizes or identifies the women at Jezebel's as radical, not fitting within the ostensible role conformity of the system but nonetheless, as 'truants' (247) (a school girlish phrase for rebellious behaviour), yet within the now stretched categories of what women can be in Gilead. The existence of prostitutes, high class call girls, escorts, on the one hand contradicts the strictly imposed regime of roles and identification of sex with procreation, and on the other hand illustrates how power can oppress the powerless and offer freedoms to the powerful, and how even the most powerful in Gilead can get away with paying lip service to the fundamental beliefs of the system. The episode contributes to the book's discussions about power, roles for women, and individual freedom.

When the Commander asks her to act naturally for their own safety, this reminds Offred that as a woman in such situations she is meant to be silent and compliant. 'All you have to do, I tell myself, is keep your mouth shut and look stupid. It shouldn't be that hard' (247). The voice in her head echoes stereotypical views about women (ornamental, stupid, silent, compliant). It is an interesting situation since the Commander also emphasizes his sense of his own power, through the breaking of rules. In the republic, as in all situations of power, those in complete control can subvert the rules which imprison others. In this small situation Offred realizes he can show off, enjoy his power, but the language with which this is described emphasizes its childish play, its performance; he's taking risks. No one in power is as infallible as they think themselves to be in such a game playing, rule breaking situation as described here. Noting Offred's critique and ironic description, the reader cannot but feel how very hypocritical the regime is, hypocritical and very dangerous, because while it has a stranglehold on how women behave, and tortures and murders those men or women who do not conform, the loopholes are there for people in power. The rich and powerful can always steer a way through the rules they themselves enforce on others.

> It occurs to me he is showing off. He is showing me off, to them, and they understand that, they are decorous enough, they keep their hands to themselves, but they review my breasts, my legs, as if there's no reason why they shouldn't. But also he is showing off to me. He is demonstrating, to me, his mastery of the world. He's breaking the rules, under their noses, thumbing his nose at them, getting away with it. Perhaps he's reached that state of intoxication which power is said to inspire, the state in which you believe you are indispensable and can therefore do anything, absolutely anything you feel like, anything at all. Twice, when he thinks no one is looking, he winks at me.
>
> It's a juvenile display, the whole act, and pathetic; but it's something I understand. (248)

Offred has seen this behaviour before. It both emphasizes gendered power play, and also emphasizes the power play between those who have and those who do not have the power. This play undercuts any righteousness, which those in power might insist accompanies their roles. It leads her into thinking about how women are expected to play a variety of performative roles to suit the needs of men, something which Gilead frees them from, as it also removes their freedoms – an irony: 'Nature demands variety, for men' (249), the Commander insists on this as a truth, and women comply, he argues, naturally (a 'natural' response which is insisted on here of course not merely by economics, but by force and on pain of being sent to the colonies). Women knew that instinctively, 'Why did they buy so many different clothes, in the old days? To trick the men into thinking they were several different women. A new one each day' (249). This is a phrase which Atwood herself has used elsewhere in order to talk about how she changes what she wears, very aware of the need to perform different roles to please this male need for variety. However, her awareness of the need and deliberate compliance with it means she is actually in control of it (which the women in Gilead are not). The Commander fails to see her ironic response ' "so now that we don't have different clothes" I say, "you merely have different women" ' (249).

Moira, when spotted, looks like a Playboy bunny, in an ill fitting rabbit suit, tatty, staggering on shoes which are too old and too big. Replaying their school girlish exchanges and time at the Red Centre, Offred goes to meet her secretly in the Ladies.

Chapter 38

The Ladies is as it was in the days when Jezebel's was a hotel, but now it is also a sanctuary for women to smoke, take off their shoes, relax, check what they look like (in the only mirrors in Gilead, it seems) and bond. The novel fills in the narrative about Moira, who represents an alternative, a radical energy. Offred and Moira catch up with details of Moira's escape and decision to become a working girl rather than be sent to the colonies. All around them, however, are the signs that everyone is performing a role. 'This is like backstage: greasepaint, smoke, the materials of illusion' (254). The women are pretending to be attractive for the men who have hired them, and Moira comments on the smudged version of Offred; 'You look like the Whore of Babylon' (254), emphasizing a biblical version of the role of over dressed, working, hired woman which Offred has ironically been turned into through her trip with the Commander. Knowing how to act is more generally a form of self preservation and escape. Moira's own escape from the Red Centre was aided by the way she copied Aunt Elizabeth's walk. It was also aided by the investment of religious radicals, in this case by the support and personal bravery of the Quakers and other religious couples. Atwood is not attacking or undercutting religion per se in this novel, but instead is exposing the ways in which extreme fundamentalist regimes can be dangerously excessive, blinkered, destructive. The punitive religious oppression in Gilead resembles ways in which the oppressive regimes of the past separated and punished religious non conformists such as Quakers, Puritans, Catholics, ironically many of whom fled injustice in Europe to settle in America. Such repression of religious non conformists resembles that of others who do not fit in, in terms of race and politics. Moira was passed covertly from family to family, and in doing so she discovered an 'Underground Femaleroad', which is the remains of, or in the form of, the historical Underground Railroad. This was a human escape route which Harriet Tubman used to enable African-American slaves in the nineteenth century to move from the south, where slavery continued, to the north where it had been first abolished. This references Offred's radical activity, even in a situation of control amid abuse. Although Moira was eventually betrayed and taken to Jezebel's (the alternative was to pick over nuclear waste in the colonies), this is testimony to an underground which has alternative views and could enable some to escape. This is a positive and wonderful piece of information for Offred, confirming some of the hints about a resistance movement which she has gained from the first Ofglen. However, what has happened to Moira saddens Offred, who needs her friend to be a model, energetic, alternative, radical like a pirate, 'swashbuckling' (261), while instead in her friend's voice she hears 'indifference'. Offred worries that while Moira must be a hero for her, to free her imagination and spirit, nonetheless she herself has been squashed by the violence she must have met on being recaptured, and her spirit quietened by the lack of choices. Moira points out the fate of women who don't fit one of Gilead's roles. For instance, old women are considered valueless in a society which only values fertility and they are sent to the colonies, so there are no old women around. In the colonies, picking through the nuclear waste, no one lasts long. Moira rises above the demeaning and oppressive situation to some extent. She declares her sexual choice as lesbian, and describes the place as a 'butch paradise' (261) but Offred feels saddened by her situation, and says she would like to tell us a positive story but can't, as she never saw Moira again. This chapter provides Moira's story of escape and incarceration, and offers a contribution to the ongoing theme of the need to make sense of one's life through framing and telling stories which manage the otherwise confusing and unmanageable. Offred likes and needs to construct stories and versions of people to make sense of her life and the world. 'Here is what I'd like to tell. I'd like to tell a story about how Moira escaped, for good this time. Or if I couldn't tell that, I'd like to say she blew up Jezebel's, with fifty Commanders inside it. I'd like to end with something daring and spectacular, some outrage . . . ' (262) but 'I never saw her again'. (262)

Chapter 39

Power, sexuality, storytelling continue as themes in this chapter. Here Moira's story of the last time she saw Offred's mother and Offred's surprised discovery that her mother's flat had been ransacked, her things broken, and that her mother had disappeared, alternates with her sad, desperate and 'inert' relationship with the Commander. Jezebel's is the hotel she and Luke used to meet in. The contrast between the time she and Luke were lovers in this hotel – when the luxury of bath soap and towels related to their love making – with her tired, glitzy, crumpled, experience now, is very sad. It emphasizes her terrible loss of love, relationships, meaning, value. The Commander seems to have hoped that bringing her there at the moment when she was sexually fertile would lead to love making rather than the regimented act of the Ceremony. Offred is ovulating, it is the day before the day of the Ceremony. The Commander is playing with his power, her freedom, in this hotel now used as a brothel and with rooms for hire for lovers. He clearly felt that the context would enable them to have sex together in a meaningful relationship, but the situation is in contrast to his misplaced hope. Offred has been taken there, she has no free will and, although she sometimes views him as a pleasant person, she does not love him. This emptiness is emphasized by the contrast with the love of the past, the forced compliance contrasted with the radical freedom of slipping away to be with Luke when they were in love and had free choice, and the dangers of non compliance emphasized in her memory of her mother's rooms being ransacked and her being sent, it seems, to the colonies. There is no possibility of free choice and love in a situation of power, force and oppression, with such differences of position between Offred and the Commander.

XIII. Night

Chapter 40

On returning from the evening at Jezebel's where the Commander has been behaving illicitly, Offred now has to fit in with Serena Joy's plans. The Wife wants a child and her plot is to use Offred and Nick to produce one, in case the Commander is sterile. Serena Joy's accompaniment of Offred to Nick's room, in the dark with the searchlights out, could be an example of women working together, except that there is loathing on the Wife's part, and Offred feels used, manipulated, endangered. Offred tells us all that happens to her but she also acknowledges how people construct versions of events, tell tales, write within conventions. So she gives us various versions of her meeting with Nick. She notes how each of these is a fictional version, described within and using the conventions of romantic fictions of various kinds. The first version is sensual and exciting, he is 'a man made of darkness . . . love, it's been so long, I'm alive in my skin, again, arms around him, falling and water softly everywhere . . . I made that up. It didn't happen that way. Here is what happened' (273). This refusal of the first version from a romantic fiction genre, and substitution of a second version unsettles the reader but emphasizes how we tell ourselves stories and cope with events by shaping them in familiar narrative forms.

The second version suggests that their sexual activity is rushed and even clinical. Their conversation is filled with clever remarks and clichés, as in the movies, but they are – in this version – aware of the way in which they are performing established roles and using worn, artificial, clichéd language. This undercuts any version of romantic talk in the movies: 'Possibly nobody ever talked like that in real life, it was all a fabrication from the beginning. Still, it's amazing how easily it comes back to mind, this corny and falsely gay sexual banter. I can see now what it's for, what it was always for: to keep the core of yourself out of reach, enclosed, protected' (274). These are only ways in which people relate to each other; the hackneyed phrases they use are all recognizably performances, and the result is some kind of self protection because feelings are never discussed. This set of comments is a contribution to the novel's discussion of themes of identity, the questioning and performance of versions of self. This scene too, however, is also a construction. Offred tells us this and in so doing is acknowledging the impossibility of expressing the complexities of reality, of life, in words. In particular, she notes: 'All I can hope for is a reconstruction: the way love feels is always only approximate' (275). She realizes that she is thinking about Luke, guilt, shame, her own need for interaction with another, her awareness of pretence, her loss; it is a hollow feeling which contrasts with the vitality of the sensuality. So there are several versions and a standing back, which empties the scene out of emotion and energy. Like Offred, the reader cannot ever know what the moment was really like, and it is suggested that this is true beyond this moment, since everything we tell ourselves and others is always only a story, a construction.

QUESTIONS

1. How do these chapters deal with issues of the relationship between sex and power?
2. How does the telling of Moira's story contribute to the novel's exploration of freedom, oppression and choice?
3. How and why does Offred emphasize the ways in which she and others construct versions of events, tell stories? To what effect?

XIV. Salvaging

Chapter 41

This is the last major section of the novel and so both furthers
and rounds off some of the issues and themes with which the rest
of the novel has been dealing. It also leaves a great many questions unanswered, both about Offred's life, and about the kinds
of issues which are explored throughout the novel. These include
debates about gender roles and their freedom or performativity,
the constraints and the role of power for both men and women.
Truth telling, the importance of storytelling and its relationship
to reality also continues as a concern. Offred continues to discuss her role as narrator, this time directly addressing the reader
and apologizing for the kind of story she is telling, its shortcomings, its lack of focus and direction. She says she wishes 'it were
about love, or about sudden realizations important to one's life'
(279). Although she acknowledges that, in a sense, it can be all
about these things, it is cluttered with everyday detail. Indeed,
such cluttering resembles any story telling about reality rather
than a fictional narrative. Recording reality, which she claims
she is doing here, produces a more cluttered and less formed
product than a formal narrative with a beginning, middle and
end and a message to be conveyed. This acknowledgement of the
shortcomings of the tale, however, only serves to highlight the
ways in which it is focused and passes on messages about identity, forms and functions of storytelling to make sense of reality,
worth and power. Talking directly to us, Offred feels a compulsion to tell her tale and indicates she would like us to share ours
with her if we can ever meet. This draws the reader in, as if our
stories were also interesting and as if knowing hers, we would
be implicated, we would need to do something about it. We are
spoken to in an immediate fashion, although, of course Offred's
tale comes from the future, placing us as readers in a more distant future which takes place both after Offred and after the
discovery of the tapes on which her tale was recorded. The compulsion to tell and hear and then to consider what to do next, is
very strong: ' . . . I keep on going with this sad and hungry and
sordid, this limping and mutilated story, because after all I want
you to hear it, as I will hear yours too if I ever get the chance,
if I meet you or if you escape . . .' (279). In this latter comment,

she assumes we must also be in some form of imprisonment. In telling stories and assuming an audience or reader Offred confirms her own existence: 'I believe you're there, I believe you into being. Because I'm telling you this story I will your existence. I tell, therefore you are' (279). As such, Offred's tale and Atwood's novel about this future oppressive regime, contribute to ongoing discussions about the role of fiction, and of storytelling, the importance of communication, being heard so that value can be debated, individual experience validated and recognized, and the importance of humanity confirmed. So in another context Anne Frank's diary offered readers insights into the life of an ordinary Jewish girl under the Nazi regime, a version of the life of someone who otherwise would have been utterly erased and denied.

The tale Offred goes on to tell is one of repeated visits to Nick, a tale of love, lust, or sex sought out because it is possible each time that there will never be a future, no further opportunities. The place they meet, in Nick's room, is important as a location for their love, and she memorizes each element of him while, sadly, her less focused memory of Luke starts to fade. But in so doing, she is aware that this seemingly most safe place, safe because they are close, is also the most dangerous, because their love is illegal in Gilead. 'Being here with him is safety; it's a cave, where we huddle together while the storm goes on outside. This is a delusion, of course. This room is one of the most dangerous places I could be. If I were caught there would be no quarter, but I'm beyond caring' (281–2). Their relationship is life affirming for both of them, but particularly for Offred, but it also makes her reckless because meeting Nick is utterly dangerous and would lead to banishment and death if they were caught. She tells Nick her real name which both indicates an involvement of her inner self, her identity and is also dangerous since now he has access to part of her which he could betray, and she has betrayed something of herself through giving her name away. The potential for destruction is clear when she comments on the flowers, which she notices occasionally and significantly through the novel (Serena Joy snipping off seedpods, heady flowers at night). She notes: 'the flowers of high summer: daisies, black-eyed Susans, starting us on the long downward slope to fall' (282).

In terms of the development of the journey of the story, it is clear she is taking risks and will be caught. Even in describing the waning summer flowers, the language hints at a loss of innocence, a loss of focus, a loss of taking safety precautions, and reminds us of the first Fall, a biblical reference of Eve being tempted by the snake and Adam choosing to follow her, both being sent from the Garden of Eden, their Fall leading to human guilt and punishment. It is also a reminder of a falling in love, a version of Offred's feelings for Nick which also more clearly resemble an obsessive longing, blotting out all other concerns. The regime under which she lives has so removed all everyday relationships that this obsession replaces her natural focus of choice: 'Such seriousness about a man, then, had not seemed possible to me before' (283). Ofglen's attempts to get her to find out more about the Commander are completely overlooked by Offred – as if she were in a haze which blocks out everything else, because of her relationship.

Chapter 42

This chapter also opens with threatening hints. 'The bell is tolling' (284) is both a call to the district Salvaging and a threat, a death toll, a warning to Offred in relation to the end of her current state of stolen pleasure. The Salvaging is actually a staged event in which women's crimes are punished. In a parallel scene to the weddings of the Prayvaganza, this celebratory moment offers the opportunity to see what happens to those who do not, or will not, fit into the demands of the regime. The contrast between the setting, which is a reminder of previous days of free speech and study, and the event of punishment, is emphasized by the location. It is set in the grounds of Harvard with the library, dormitories and other academic buildings, now run by the Eyes and so closed, their window blinds drawn as if blind eyes, keeping out questions and truths. The three women who are to be punished are two Handmaids and a Wife. 'All of them sit on folding wooden chairs, like graduating students who are about to be given prizes' (285) –an ironic contrast with their punishment. The chapter is filled with such contrast and also seems to be building towards a climax. The setting is ironically performative, artificial, as the occupants of the stage light up with the sun 'like a Christmas crèche'

(286). The reappearance of Aunt Lydia also reminds us of the opening of the novel when the women were being trained as Handmaids. This is the punishment for those who stray and Aunt Lydia's speech is filled with platitudes, slogans and clichés about 'the torch of the future, the cradle of the race, the task before us' (286). The change in this Salvaging – an ironic term which suggests salvation but means death – is that the crimes are not going to be read out because such an identification of potential crimes or deviances stimulated the women's imaginations in the past and they lost control over their feelings. The impossibility of imaginative escape is emphasized in the probable crime of the Wife who is to be killed. She perhaps tried adultery, abortion or escape – each equally impossible. The women are hanged. Their deaths are meant as cautionary tales but also ways of forcing a unity against deviance. As if to join in their response to the others, the Handmaids have to reach forward and touch the ropes and show unity with their hands on their hearts.

Chapter 43

The scene of the Salvaging continues, lingering on the dead bodies. Offred uses irony to point out the discrepancy between the dainty twitching shoes of the women and their hanged, hooded bodies. 'They look arranged. They look like showbiz' (289). It is a performance, artificial but deadly, which perspective undercuts the seriousness of the event but also emphasizes its danger for Offred since it is very real, and her own dangerously deviant behaviour could lead to her being the next victim. The violence of the day is not over, however, and as with other oppressive regimes, collusion and joint violence is now sought. The women are asked to form an orderly circle and then they then experience a Particicution which resembles an execution but is actually a way of enabling them to let off steam with violent abuse towards a man who is accused of rape. The man is drugged and like the three hanged women he cannot defend himself verbally or in any other way. The hatred that the women feel for men's control over their bodies and rights, coupled with this particular crime, rape – an invasion of their sexual selves – forms a torrent of loathing and a desire for blood: ' . . . there is a bloodlust; I want to tear, gouge, rend' (291). Atwood's comic touch is uppermost even in this violent and unpleasant collusive scene, exposing it, undercutting the power behind it. Farcically, Aunt Lydia controls their violent anger with the whistle previously used in volleyball games. This is out of place in a group murder, but emphasizes the grotesqueness of the scene and the farce of a staged opportunity for brutality for those whose other emotions are utterly controlled. Under such totalitarian control, all their emotions hemmed in, the venting of any emotion is dangerous. The women turn into beasts. So we see that in situations of little choice, violence and inhumane behaviour emerge, which is an indictment against any oppressive regime where people cannot have the freedom to understand right and wrong and make their own choices.

The condemned man seems drunk, his face pulped. He denies the crime but no one could possibly hear this above the noise; 'he has become an *it*' (292) emphasizing the dehumanization. Ofglen's pointed kick to his head puts him out of his misery and saves him the pain of being mutilated. She was aware that he was not a rapist, that the scene had been a set up to punish a political crime.

For Janine, this is another step towards madness and regression back into her role as a waitress. But Offred feels no sympathy. The death makes Offred feel real – another alarming response; she wants to make love, or eat a horse. It makes her feel that she is alive, in contrast to his death. This is of course socially a dangerous contrast, but her first person testimony illustrates to us how easy it is for anyone to get caught up in the rhythm of the regime and take part in unthinkable acts of violence despite their own inner sense that such involvement is wrong.

Chapter 44

The first statement – 'things are back to normal' (294) –feels bizarre in the circumstances. The sense of complacency however is disrupted when Offred realizes that her shopping companion is now a 'new' Ofglen, which leaves her worrying about what has happened to her friend, the radical, original

Ofglen. The change is a shock and Offred is disturbed. Not knowing how to test the values of this replacement she is less cautious than previously, probably because of her careless state. The change emphasizes ways in which individuality is removed: 'I never did know her real name. That is how you can get lost, in a sea of names. It wouldn't be easy to find her, now' (295). The women are reduced to only their functions and named according to whom they serve. In trying to interpret her coded language, Offred is confused. If the hanging women are a reminder to them, what is it a reminder of? The need for obedience, or a warning about possible betrayal in an unjust regime? The duplicity of language and the power it has over people is clear in this brief exchange and Offred has to become alert. However, she realizes that while the new Ofglen is not one of the radicals (among whom she now numbers herself) she, Offred, knows of their existence, which is dangerous. Ofglen tells her that the previous Ofglen hung herself. This chapter is a very important change moment. It emphasizes Offred's vulnerability. Used and given extra freedoms by Serena Joy, the Commander and Nick, she is both more herself, less dulled by the endless constraint and focus, but also more vulnerable.

Chapter 45

The power of a regime lies in its control, the way in which it can dominate identity, the mind and the body, language and any form of the individual's sense of ownership and choice. Offred, feeling released from terror through Ofglen's suicide, is so grateful that the morning feels new and she would willingly just conform to keep herself safe and alive. Changing perception is concentrated on in several places in the book. Earlier, Aunt Lydia said that they would get used to their new lack of freedom, their roles, that they would forget the past, that they would in the future not even expect certain lifestyles, things, the opportunity to read, make choices about jobs, money, relationships. So, in the years to come, future generations would not have the difficulties that they had because they would know no other way, know no better. As soon as bank accounts were frozen for women and women were no longer allowed to own money or have jobs, Offred noticed a shift in the power relationship with Luke, that unwittingly and unintentionally he could decide to care for her because he had the power to do so (or not care for her, should he want that, since it was all in his power). Paternalism, fatherly care, is also a product of dominant, oppressive male control, and patriarchy – each is an element in the ways in which power dictates its laws to language, sexuality, identity, freedom. In her relationship with Nick, Offred realised that she has changed her perception of male/female relationships to one of dependency and necessity and that relationships with men are the absolute cornerstone of her life, where previously they were just one element. Her freedom of language is also constantly under threat. Even the interpretation of the limited, coded responses of the Handmaids has been made dangerous and untrustworthy, first when Offred was unaware of the interpretation to put on the vacuous obedient religious phrases which she and the first Ofglen had to mutter to each other on their shopping walk, and then – when Ofglen was replaced by the new Ofglen – the same phrase would be understood differently, misinterpreted in a dangerous way.

Just to stay alive, Offred would now do anything – the power over her is so great. The regime has at least temporarily reinstated its full control over her:

> 'I don't want to be a doll hung up on the Wall, I don't want to be a wingless angel. I want to keep on living, in any form. I resign my body freely, to the uses of others. They can do what they like with me. I am abject.
> I feel, for the first time, their true power.' (298)

Serena Joy confronts her with the stained cloak, and both of them realize that she knows that Offred went out with the Commander. Although she is being treated here as a naughty, disobedient teenager, Offred of course had no choice in the matter; she is caught and seen as guilty in a triangular relationship where both the Commander and his Wife have control over her body and her actions: 'Just like the other one, a slut' (299) is Serena Joy's comment. This is a decisive comment but Offred had no alternative and there is no one to help her.

XV. Night

Chapter 46

The titles of this section suggests darkness, threat, and indeed it is the end of life in the Commander's home in Gilead for Offred because the many rules she has broken are beginning to add up against her. The end of dreams is indicated in her description: 'I sit in my room, at the window, waiting. In my lap is a handful of crumpled stars' (303). These are stars perhaps from the dress she wore when visiting Jezebel's but they also indicate lost hopes and dreams and as she plays with words – being in waiting, in disgrace as the opposite of grace – she indicates loss. She is as if under suspension in a job, and in suspense over what will happen next; it is a pause. The short shape of the sentences suggests someone who is waiting for the end, almost dissociated from her emotions. It gets darker, not only because of night but because she fears what happens next, and again Offred contemplates suicide or fire starting – 'A signal of some kind to mark my exit' (304) because so many people just disappear, and she feels she will too. She examines words, such as fatigue and faith, and considers forms of death. The final part of her time here is terrifying – the arrival of the black van threatens death, extinction and pain. The van comes to take her away as traditionally it took prisoners and the insane, and the bell tolling represents death; referencing a ghost indicates how she feels that her identity will be snuffed out. Paying attention and taking things into her own hands are all meant literally here. If she had a sharp weapon the choice of suicide would, she feels, be better than being imprisoned and brutally punished.

'As I'm standing up I hear the black van. I hear it before I see it; blended with the twilight, it appears out of its own sound like a solidification, a clotting of the night. It turns into the driveway, stops. I can just make out the white eye, the two wings. The paint must be phosphorescent. Two men detach themselves from the shape of it, come up the front steps, ring the bell. I hear the bell toll, ding-dong, like the ghost of a cosmetics woman, down in the hall.

Worse is coming then.

I've been wasting my time. I should have taken things into my own hands while I had the chance. I should have stolen a knife from the kitchen, found some way to the sewing scissors. There were the garden shears, the knitting needles; the world is full of weapons if you're looking for them. I should have paid attention.' (305)

But Nick alerts her that it is all right, the people are 'Mayday' – the revolutionary group, and as she is escorted out and Serena Joy and the Commander look on aghast, the reader hopes that Offred will survive (and indeed she must have survived or we would never have her testimony in the novel – or perhaps it survived her, since it was found many years in the future). We can only speculate about what actually happens to her. This closure of the tale, the end of Offred, leaves us wondering what will happen next, as she does. The language used suggests either a kind of heavenly ascendance, an escape, or entry into something dark and heartrending; the refusal to tell us leaves us wondering.

'And so I step up, into the darkness within; or else the light'. (307)

HISTORICAL NOTES

Here the story of Offred is established as both real and historical. By placing discussion of its discovery and historical relevance in an academic framework Offred is not finished when her story ended for us because the story itself was discovered and has formed part of a way of interpreting a moment in history. Atwood emphasizes the academic notes, context, all the elements of research which establish the tale as real, while simultaneously questioning its authenticity as scholarship tends to do, and the interpretation of its significance within the frame of the academic reading offered by Professor James Darcy Pieixoto at the Twelfth Symposium of Gileadean Studies in 2195.

The Professor's name – Darcy – recalls Mr Darcy, the romantic hero in Jane Austen's *Pride and Prejudice* and is fitting for a story in which romance is frustrated and longed for, and its basis located in male power and ownership. However, romantic fictions and their values and historical study both expose the roles and values of Gilead, which are all problematized. The Professor is probably of Latin American or similar descent so the exclusiveness of Gilead has been overturned. And the list of conference activities – walks, shows, costumes and sing songs which attempt to recreate an authentic version of Gilead for the conference goers serves to emphasize the artificial, the performativity which was also common throughout life in Gilead in the novel. The conference seems trivial in the light of Offred's disappearance and our closeness as readers to her thoughts and her fate. But it also reassures us that her tale survived and that the dreadful controls of Gilead passed on, that human nature can survive such mind and body control and destruction. The comparison with Iran betrays Atwood's initial influences, seeing women in the Burka, all in black, defined by their marital status and denied freedom of education (this was the case when she began the novel, but is not necessarily true of all of Iran in the early twenty-first century). Pieixoto's speech labels and defines the context of the discovery of the tapes, which are found in an American footlocker; this is amusing as it would normally hold gym shoes but instead holds Offred's tale. The tapes were found in Bangor, Maine, part of the Underground Femaleroad or Frailroad (a joke version, hinting at women's frailty) which also proves that such a railroad or escape system was real because it is now identified as a context, and its origins explained. However, we are very aware that history and scholars interpret and represent what they see according to their own contexts and intentions so anything the Professor says is an interpretation, probably selective, limited, misrepresented. Offred's tale is also identified as a heroic monument of sorts from the Republic of Gilead period, by being compared with other tales which have been unearthed and which testify to other activities in different times and places. Pieixoto and his colleague, Professor Wade, have reconstructed a tape machine, with the aid of a technician, so that they could play the tapes. But they have also arranged the blocks of the speech so that what we have in the end, is *The Handmaid's Tale*, named after Chaucer's *Canterbury Tales*. The

pun on 'tail' suggests it is something arranged by male scholars, something of an irony given that the testimony is from
a woman and about her constrained life under a totalitarian,
religious patriarchally dominated tyranny. Their information
and authority also undercuts the authenticity of Offred's voice:
'Obviously, it could not have been recorded during the period
of time it recounts' (315) he tells us, since Offred would not
have had access to a tape machine, so it is perhaps authentic
but recorded at a different moment. The intentions of Offred
are unknown and there are few details of her.

Like all unearthed relics and manuscripts, the intention,
context and aims, quality of the context and authorship are
questionable. They cannot trace Offred but place her as one
of the first, recruited for reproductive purposes. They place
her tale in the historical context of a post holocaust disaster, where biological warfare stocks were dumped into the
sewage system and insecticides and other pollutants all com-
bined to make the place toxic. Here we get a context which
is aligned with Atwood's writing against pollution and her
interest in sustainability. Even the Commander is placed historically as someone who spoke against enabling women to
read. He is quoted as saying, 'our big mistake was teaching
them to read. We won't do that again' (320). Names are given,
fact runs through. All of Offred's life and times are places
for us. Somehow this both authenticates her story – she did
live, these things did happen – and yet places some doubt
on its ability to comment on everything because writing is
seen as affected by time, place and the writer as well as the
ability for the readers to interpret; we have come so close to
her thoughts and experiences that the distancing and rather
sterile, nosy exploration of her life and works by academics
seems an intrusion. This is of course also ironic, since such a
piecing together and speculating is exactly what we are doing
in reading and discussing the book ourselves. Pieixoto sounds
a note which suggests he is more interested in the sound of
his own eloquence than in Offred's fate, but as readers this
puts into a sharp perspective our very focused interest in her
fate, and in the truth of what she wrote. It also contributes
to the debate throughout about performance (the audience
applause) and constructedness.

QUESTIONS

1. How does the story gather momentum towards its climax and end?
2. What are the particular roles of the Salvaging and the Particicution in terms of the novel's debates about power, sexuality, language and individuality?
3. How does placing the tale historically, as if of academic interest, contribute to the novel's discussions of power, language, gender, interpretation, or any other theme which is of interest to you?

CHAPTER 4

RECEPTION AND INFLUENCE

This chapter provides an overview of critical reception from initial reviews to current critical approaches.

RANGE, KIND AND TIMING OF CRITICAL RESPONSES

Atwood's novels always receive a range of critical comments immediately upon publication, in the form of international and local reviews. Essays follow in journals, and there are a number of notable critics who have been working on her entire oeuvre or life work, and who eagerly await a new novel in order to discuss how and where it fits in with the others or deviates from them. Years after its publication *The Handmaid's Tale* remains a favourite not only for study but also for critical discussion, testimony to the topicality of its debates about rights, power, sexuality, language, identity.

DYSTOPIA AND SCIENCE FICTION

Critics have explored the novel in a variety of ways since its publication. Some discuss it as a feminist text that debates issues of reproductive technology and women's roles, while others consider it a dystopia which focuses on religion and power, where Gilead is a religious fundamentalist regime. The latter often identify images and critique reminiscent of Big Brother in George Orwell's *Nineteen Eighty-four* (1948) who watched and heard everything anyone did or thought, and Aldous Huxley's dystopia of *Brave New World* (1932), in which reproductive technology is commonplace, science rules and the arts are seen as primitive and nonconformist.

Local reviewer Ken Adachi (*The Sunday Star,* 29 September 1985, 'Atwood's Futuristic Fiction') describes the book as 'intense, compelling' noting its 'quiet intense hypnotic' grip comparing it as satire, Sufi and theology: 'one might call this a feminist theological novel; certainly it is didactic, densely infiltrated by myth, metaphor and history. Swift's *A Modest Proposal* the Biblical Genesis, Orwell's *Nineteen Eighty-four* and other dystopias' are comparable, as are Doris Lessing's 'energetic satires on the totalitarian state as viewed from outer space' (p. G11).

Atwood has also made many critical statements about her work, as well as speaking of its origins. It is important not to take everything an author says as the final word on critical interpretation since, for example, authors often deliberately do not engage with cultural issues, which we might read or see in their work, or are unaware they are revealing values, points of view. Nonetheless, her comments about intention, reception, and the effects of the studying and reading of the novel are fascinating, and an exploration of the archives containing her work, in the Thomas Fisher rare book library of the University of Toronto, reveals much about her intentions and response to the reception by others. Atwood is very clear about the effect of the work of Orwell and Huxley on her own thoughts and her novel, but, she argues, it is not a piece of science fiction, because,

> the seeds of everything it contains lie in the reality around us. . . . it certainly isn't science fiction. Science fiction is filled with Martians and space travel to other planets, and things like that. That isn't this book at all. *The Handmaid's Tale* is speculative fiction in the genre of *Brave New World* and *Nineteen Eighty-four*. *Nineteen Eighty-four* was written not as science fiction but as an extrapolation of life in 1948. So, too, *The Handmaid's Tale* is a slight twist on the society we have now. (An Interview with Margaret Atwood on her novel *The Handmaid's Tale*)

Scholars of science fiction, however, might well debate her limited version of its definition, suggesting instead that the transfer into the future or elsewhere of issues common today is precisely what much science fiction does, causing us to reflect on our lives and maybe take action. Kate Fullbrook (1990) sees *The Handmaid's Tale* as a dystopian feminist novel, a version of science fiction, building on Huxley's *Brave New World* (1932), and

Orwell's *Nineteen Eighty-four* (see Cathy Davidson's review, 1986).

WOMEN'S ROLES, MEN'S ROLES AND FEMINISM

Feminist critics and readers have both celebrated and argued over the book. It offers a contradictory picture of sisterhood, translating into the future context some of the best held beliefs of second wave feminism, exposing their flaws. Reproductive value is all, in Gilead, replacing the dangers of rape and pornography. But reduction to separated roles for women and an emphasis on reproduction limits functions, disempowers and silences the different women of Gilead. Despite the new safety for women and the removal of any need for one woman to be carrying all the female roles at once; in other words, being a form of superwoman as wife, mother, hostess mistress; nonetheless, the situation for woman is actually far worse in Gilead than in twentieth-century America. Male power forcefully re-emerges in its different forms, and women are denied the opportunity or right to own money, property, jobs or their own reproductive systems.

But although her work does not merely reproduce the assertions and values of feminism, Atwood does acknowledge its impact. She says in an interview conducted by Ellen Coughlin in *Books and Arts* (7 March 1980, p. 6) 'I think it is ridiculous for any woman in my position, who writes books and is a professional, to say she's *not* a feminist. I don't believe women who've been to school and have been to college and have jobs and then say they aren't feminists, because their whole mode of existence has been made possible by people several generations ago who chained themselves to fences. If feminism is dealing with women as independent entities, then I'm a feminist'. She is not a propagandist for the movement, however, and takes some of its visions and claims literally to highly contradictory conclusions.

Looking at the novel's power to challenge dystopian forms and to produce an opinion of history, specifically that of the silenced, Coral Ann Howells comments:

Atwood's version focuses on what has traditionally been left out of the dystopia. Offred, the Handmaid in Gilead, is marginalized and disempowered because of her sex, so that her story shifts the structural relation between the private and public worlds of the dystopia, where the officially silenced Other becomes the central narrative voice, displacing the grand narratives of the Bible and official Gileadean history. This is *history,* a deconstructive view of patriarchal authority, which in turn is challenged at an academic conference two hundred years later by the male Cambridge historian Professor Pieixoto, who tries to discredit Offred's version for its lack of documentary information. However, by this time Offred has the author's support (in the pun "Denay Nunavit") and she also has the reader's sympathy, so that history does not succeed in undermining history after all. (Howells, C. A. (2000) 'Transgressing Genre: A Generic Approach to Margaret Atwood's Novels: *The Handmaid's Tale* and Dystopia' in Nischik, R. M. (ed.) *Margaret Atwood: Works and Impact*, Rochester: Camden House, p. 142)

It is a particularly female form of the dystopian novel, not merely because of its focus on a single woman, Offred, and her experiences in the totalitarian and divisive state, but because of its leaking of a dissident and denied voice, and one which expresses feelings about the body, and about women's experiences:

> We might conclude that *The Handmaid's Tale* is a dissident dystopia, though it cannot be reduced to that generic classification. Though it shares many of the thematic features of traditional models of the genre, it subverts the masculine dystopian fascination with institutional politics or military tactics by focusing on the silenced Others in Gilead. Likewise, Offred's story with all its gaps and confessions of unreliability challenges Professor Pieixoto's deterministic view of history and the role of historiography as authentication of the past, in favour of something far more arbitrary and subjectively reconstructed. (Howells, C. A. (2000) in Nischik, R. M. p. 143)

Current criticism often focuses on a critique of reproductive technology, however concerns and issues of second wave feminism explored in the novel are themselves a focus of critique.

Sisterhood, communities of women and a world free of rape and male violence are feminist ideals but the roles for women in Gilead are prescribed, women are set against each other and fertility and reproduction are the whole measure of women's worth. In a very English interpretation, Lorna Sage (*Times Literary Supplement*, 21 March 1986, 'Projections from a Messy Present') at the beginning of the critical response, recognizes its mixed feminist message:

> One of the book's persistent polemical projections is the tendency in present day feminism towards a kind of separatist pit, a matriarchal nostalgia (Offred's mother, we discover, went it alone – 'A man is just a woman's strategy for making other women', burned pornographic magazines, reclaimed the night) that seems to combine with the language of conservation and 'back to Nature'. This in turn, threatens to join forces with right-wing demands for 'traditional values', law and order, national and racial chauvinism. (Sage, 1986, p. 307)

Sage likes Moira less and feels she is unconvincing. She also critiques the ex-market researcher, mildly perverse Commander, commenting that surely even patriarchal male sexuality can't feel this strange? Sage notes that Offred has acknowledged that future readers could be male: 'Offred's most difficult task is to persuade herself that her eventual reader – her real partner in crime – may be a man . . . . This gnomic stuff is the measure of the difficulties Margaret Atwood has set herself in not only synthesizing a future (which she does, mainly, with aplomb) but putting the present together' (Sage, 1986, p. 307). She sees the strangeness culminating in a 'game of heterosexual Scrabble'.

One of Atwood's constant critics is Jane Brooks Bouson. In her analysis of *The Handmaid's Tale* she focuses on the context of the feminist backlash and the rise of the New Right. In the 1980s the New Right sought the restoration of women's traditional roles. She sees the novel as a 'feminist dystopia' (Brooks Bouson, p. 137) which contains a warning against a feminist backlash by the New Right, so the novel asks readers to consider the oppressive realities of contemporary patriarchal ideology. It challenges assumptions of male power and superiority and in so doing

> reflects on the anti-feminist messages given to women by the fundamentalist New Right in the 1980s. Atwood delineates in chilling detail just what might follow: the virtual enslavement of women, their reduction to mere functions. (Brooks Bouson, p. 135)

Brooks Bouson sees the importance of language as regulating these oppressive times:

> it also incorporates an antagonistic, feminist-dialogic speech which serves to partially contain and master the female fear it dramatizes. Describing how this tactic works, Offred muses that '[t]here is something powerful in the whispering of obscenities, about those in power . . . . It's like a spell of sorts. It deflates them, reduces them to the common denominator where they can be dealt with.' (Brooks Bouson, p. 146)

Mary McCarthy, writing soon after the book's publication, comments on Offred's feminist mother, and sees Offred's body as a swamp, taking her over. She blames the extremes of feminism for the divisiveness between women.

> 'excessive' feminism, which here seems to bear some responsibility for Gilead, to be one of its causes. The kind of doctrinaire feminism likely to produce a backlash is exemplified in the narrator's absurd mother, whom we first hear of at a book-burning in the old, pre-Gilead time – the 'right' kind of book-burning, naturally, merely a pyre of pornographic magazines: 'Mother', thinks the narrator in what has become the present, 'You wanted a women's culture. Well, now there is one.' The wrong kind, of course. (McCarthy, 1986)

LANGUAGE AND STORYTELLING

Other concerns are the trustworthiness of narrative, the partiality of what comes down to us as record, the importance of being able to develop and express an individual subjectivity.

It is recognized as a novel which explores the act of writing, first person narrative or testifying, reading and interpretation. Offred's role is a narrator constructing a tale, aware that she is reshaping events. This tale concentrates on power, controlling language and preventing free speech among the Handmaids and everyone else in Gilead. There are contradictions based in the way in which perceptions, language, interactions and all elements of people's lives are controlled, silence and social conformity enforced.

Mario Klarer (1995) uses Edward Sapir and Walter J. Ong to explore the opposition of oral and literate cultures in exploring ways in which Atwood's novel challenges the disempowerment of women in Gilead. Moving on from a similar scenario of burning books, – Ray Bradbury's influence (*Fahrenheit 451*) – Atwood has, Klarer argues, developed a gendered approach to the burning of books, the banning of reading, the enforced oral culture. She 'adopts this dichotomy of literacy and orality in a new gendered way: she depicts not only a comprehensive power structure but one which is designed to suppress women by restricting them to an oral cultural tradition'.

Atwood (1980) earlier spoke of silencing:

> In any totalitarian take-over, whether from the left or the right, writers, singers and journalists are the first to be suppressed . . . . The aim of all such suppression is to silence the voice, abolish the word, so that the only voices and words left are those of the ones in power. Elsewhere, the word itself is thought to have power; that's why so much trouble is taken to silence it. (p. 427)

In making such silencing gendered, she uses oral structures, repetition, simple sentences, listing and naming the world around her where, as in oral cultures, she feels everything takes place and is reported in *present* time always. Being able to play a word game is true freedom:

> . . . the secret games of Scrabble between the Commander and the female protagonist. Through the wooden letters of the game, literacy is literally materialized and letters can be 'touched'

'It's as if he's the letters. The feeling is voluptuous. This is freedom, an eyeblink of it.'

Accumulation and description take over from abstractism, also more conceptual thought, pictographs and labels – hoods on traitors, an ownership tag on Offred's wrist at Jezebel's – all emphasize power. However, here, Klarer notes, Atwood begins to align herself with the feminist emphasis on orality and the body.

Orality was one issue that feminist literary aesthetics re-enlisted as a means to challenge patriarchal literary discourse. Capitalizing on the way that oral discourse has been associated with the feminine – in terms of the mother-dominated domestic interaction with children and 'female gossiping' – feminists attempted to define a female mode of communication that was both an alternative and a gender-specific medium for self-expression.

We have a feminine narrative spoken on tape, challenging the script of the patriarchically controlled. Atwood refuses feminist critique of hierarchy and male power, uniting the oral and the literate in Offred's words which are nearly lost, they began as oral, taped then are scripted in a period which is longing for written works.

Language is of interest for many of the critics of the novel. Offred and the other Handmaids are forced into silence, making coded exchanges, unable to trust the words they exchange. The work of Michel Foucault (*History of Sexuality*, 1979) is useful here in relating language, sexuality and power. The regime in Gilead silences people, forces them to observe a formal discourse of compliance, using religious language. Women speak in code, any voiced dissent is both illegal and severely punished. Language is power. Women have no personal names which removes their identity; shops advertise using signs referencing biblical terms and common events are mislabelled – so 'Salvaging' is the brutal murder of dissident women and 'Particicution' is an execution, a savage putting to death of a man who, it is claimed, is a rapist. Feminists and deformed babies are treated as sub-human, called 'Unwomen' and 'Unbabies', Black and Jewish people are defined by biblical terms as 'Children of Ham' and

'Sons of Jacob'. By differentiating them from the rest of society it makes their persecution easier.

Dystopian novels often focus on repression of thought and exchange, and both *Nineteen Eighty-four* and *Brave New World* connect the political with repression. Coral Ann Howells sees *The Handmaid's Tale* as a feminist dystopian novel because of this concern with women and the body:

> Though it shares many of the thematic features of traditional models of the genre, it subverts the masculine dystopian fascination with institutional politics or military tactics by focusing on the silenced Others in Gilead. (Howells, 2000, in Nischik, R. M. (ed.) p. 143)

POWER AND FREEDOM

One of the major issues which the novel highlights is that of freedom. Lorna Sage (1986, p. 307) identifies Atwood's middle America as undermined by fanaticism and fuelled by fundamentalism. Traditional values have led to limited roles, uniforms and coded interactions in the Republic of Gilead. Everyone is under constant surveillance by the 'Eyes of God', the secret police, and open to betrayal by those they live and sleep with. It is a world where those in power behave as though they have the power of God. They hunt down 'gender traitors', gay men and lesbians and undertake constant wars against those of other religious persuasions, Baptists, Jews and Blacks (Sons of Ham), and send them for liquidation, expatriation to labour camps or transportation to the colonies to pick over toxic and radioactive waste dumps. Gilead resembles a vast garden suburb, but within a police state. John Updike (in *The New Yorker* 12 May 1986, pp. 118–25), compares attitudes and values, cultural difference when a Canadian author sets a dystopia in America and compares the North American futuristic dystopian state and the Canadian ideal, where Canada is seen by Offred and her family as a potential, free space into which to escape. The novel, he argues, focuses on the 'bemusement' of Canadians as a 'fine old northern neighbour' in the face of the 'moral strenuousness, our noisy determination to combine virtue and power, and our occasional vast miscarriages of missionary intention'

(p. 118). He is amused and surprised, that the novel is set in the now liberal Cambridge, much of it in the university of Harvard, but he is not surprised that Canada is seen as a place of escape in the early days of Gilead. Updike refuses to see the novel as a humourless feminist piece: 'This novel could have been a humourless strident tract; but the poet in the author renders it quite otherwise. The narrative is light-handed, fitful, and gradually compelling, it assembles its horrid world with a casual meditative motion, and saves most of its action for the last few pages' (p. 121). He enjoys the language and sees the pervasive pollution is being described poetically, so that the manufacture of dishcloths and smiling buttons are amusing elements which reduce the negativity and add humour. Updike says it 'does feel purposefully feminine', beneath the grim but 'playful details of its dystopia glows the vivid and intimate reality of its heroine' (p. 121). Offred's individuality and vitality prevail so he sees: 'the heroine's irrepressible vitality and the author's lovely, subversive hymn to our Orinda life as lived amid perils and pollution now' (p. 123).

Pamela Cooper uses Foucault's themes of power and surveillance to explore both overt policing through the Guardians and more menacing surveillance through the Eyes with their black vans. Pamela Cooper notes:

> *The Handmaid's Tale* thus brings together pre-Christian notions of absolute patriarchal authority – the omniscient, avenging god – with postmodernist theories of the objectifying and possessive male gaze – the omniscient, avenging eye. The proprietorial eye of male desire becomes the weapon of fascism in Gilead.

This is referenced to consider links between desire, male power and a highly sexualized observation which both treats women as objects and dismays men with fears of disempowerment and castration. The medical doctor Offred meets abuses his power:

> The unequal power dynamic here foregrounds the sinister psychology of doctor/patient relations in a society of violent gender prejudice. Offred's vulnerability is realized as the repeated experience of intrusion . . .

The film version of the book, she suggests, by dropping the tale of finding the recorded tapes in the future loses much of the irony.

RELIGIOUS FUNDAMENTALISM

Anne Kaler (1989) concentrates on the perversion of religion in Gilead which predates early twenty-first century readings of the novel as dealing with religious fundamentalism.

In a work explaining Atwood's treatment of religion, faith and merely going through the motions of piety, Nancy Workman (1989) starts by considering the third epigraph in the preface to the novel, the Sufi proverb:

> In the desert there is no sign that says,
> Thou shalt not eat stones.

Workman continues by exploring how Atwood names even the cars and shops with religious, biblical references and has Offred doubting Ofglen's prayers of piety, the effectiveness of the prayer wheel at Soul Scrolls. Workman argues that Offred asks for an inner version of a life and that this shows spirit of survival.

> The world which surrounds Offred is that of Christian fundamentalism based on biblical authority. So pervasive is the influence that even the cars which she describes have biblical Old Testament allusiveness: the Whirlwind, the Chariot, the Behemoth all possess "prestige", not only associated with their use as status symbols by their owners of various ranks, but also indicative of their owners' spiritual authority. Thus, something as innocent as a means of transportation becomes a spiritual marker, capable of hidden messages. Similarly, the shop names which identify the products for sale have New Testament allusiveness: Offred trades at the Lilies of the Field, the Milk and Honey, and the All Flesh, recalling to mind Christian parables and their rich tradition of instruction based on simple narratives. Correspondingly, the fact that these stores are frequently empty of goods attests to the fundamental emptiness of Christianity. (Workman, 1989)

Sufism also exposes language play:

> . . . like the Sufis, Offred expresses her unorthodoxy through language play, through simple statements masking complex understanding. For example, early in the novel she reveals inadequacies of patriarchal control which has not created female equivalents for certain relationships. She notes that while '*fraternize* means to behave like a brother . . . there was no corresponding word that meant *to behave like a sister*'. Offred recognizes that the discursive language of patriarchy creates its own realities by failing to name certain bonds of affectiveness that exist between women. (Workman, 1989)

There is only faith, no hope and charity here, and patriarchy dominates. Workman sees the novel as criticizing the corrupting effects of institutionalized Christianity.

Nicholson (1994) discusses the religious elements of the novel and moments from repressive early histories of America under the Puritans in the control of Cotton Mather who emphasized both the impotence and the subordination of women. Nicholson differentiates:

> One difference between the society of the novel and that of Puritan England appears at first sight absolute. For in the novel it is the lack of women with functioning ovaries which turns those who are capable of reproduction into a commodity controlled and exchanged by the men, and some women, who run this society. In colonial New England, however, the birth-rate was very high. (p. 182)

Like the Puritans, Handmaids are re-educated and re-named to indicate their ownership. Offred is named for the Commander – of Fred. Similarly, in Puritan days New England women were re-named in ways which 'providentially reminded them of their feminine destiny: Silence, Fear, Patience, Prudence, Mindwell, Comfort, Hopestill and Be Fruitful', notes Koehler. Like Atwood's Handmaids they had many 'freedoms from', such as freedom from the vanity induced by combs, mirrors and fancy clothes. They were allowed to study, but only the Bible.

Continuing a reading focusing on the religious and reproductive concerns, Sharon Wilson looks at Offred as surrogate child bearer, tracing her origins to the biblical story of Rachel and her maid Bilhah. Referencing Atwood's Professor, Northrop Frye, Wilson sees a Gileadian 'world of the nightmare and the scapegoat, of bondage, pain and confusion' (Frye, *Anatomy*, p. 147). Sharon Wilson's work traces influences and patterns, codes and archetypes. A main intertext, in terms of sexual politics, is the Biblical Genesis, but the novel also produces satires on Islam, Puritanism, Mormonism, Christianity and, particularly, contemporary fundamentalism. The biblical tale of Rachel is a clear source for *The Handmaid's Tale*. Rachel needed to bear children for Jacob, but could not, so her handmaid Bilhah fulfilled that need. As Genesis 30, 1–3, says 'she shall bear upon my knees, that I may also have children by her' (*HT* epigraph).

This range of critical responses can be augmented by looking at the books and journal articles suggested in the Chapter 5 and reading the articles and books quoted earlier. Critics engage with a range of issues in Atwood's work and in terms of this novel these have been introduced here.

CHAPTER 5

GUIDE TO FURTHER READING

There are several different kinds of further reading which you might like to undertake. You might like to read the critical works which have informed this book and others on Margaret Atwood's works, which are listed here. Some of the critical works are by critics who have followed Atwood's career over the years and have developed expert responses to her changing work. Books and essays by Coral Ann Howells are a good place to begin, followed by works of Reingard Nischik, Cathy Davidson, Harold Bloom and latterly Fiona Tolan. Much immediate response to Atwood's novels is found in the reviews, which are also discussed in Chapter 4 alongside the longer books on her work. While these books sum up her work and place the novels, short stories and poems in terms of themes, essays in journals are likely to look at Atwood's work from a particular perspective, for example, her feminist work, further autobiographical narratives or key themes. Reviews are an immediate response which try to place Atwood in relation to the times, her previous work and perceived themes. The Thomas Fisher rare book library at the University of Toronto archives Margaret Atwood's papers which means that access to notes, letters, cuttings, reviews, early drafts, holographs of manuscripts can all be requested.

You might also like to look at other books by Atwood, of which there is a select list in the chapter references below and in the suggestions for further reading. Because Atwood has written a great deal you might find you prefer work of different periods or different threads throughout her work to date. You might choose to read the earlier works which have a feminist interest in survival and in critiquing romantic myths: *Lady Oracle* (1976), *Surfacing* (1972), *The Edible Woman* (1969), or later work which uses myths again to explore women's lives,

The Robber Bride (1993), *Wilderness Tips* (1991), *Good Bones* (1992). The short stories are of more general interest and still later the fantasy, speculative, futuristic fiction which moves – as does *The Handmaid's Tale* – into the future of such as *Oryx and Crake* (2003) and *The Year of the Flood* (2009), both companions to *The Handmaid's Tale* in terms of their speculations about dystopian futures.

CHAPTER 1: CONTEXT

Atwood, Margaret, (1961), *Double Persephone*. Toronto: Hawkshead Press

Atwood, Margaret, (1966), *The Circle Game*. Bloomfield Hills, MI: Cranbrook Academy of Art

Atwood, Margaret, (1968), *The Animals in That Country*. Toronto: Oxford University Press

Atwood Margaret, (1969), *The Edible Woman*. Toronto: McClelland & Stewart

Atwood, Margaret, (1970), *The Journals of Susanna Moodie*. Toronto: Oxford University Press

Atwood, Margaret, (1970), *Procedures for Underground*. Toronto: Oxford University Press

Atwood, Margaret, (1971), *Power Politics*. Toronto: Anansi

Atwood, Margaret, (1972), *Surfacing*. Toronto: McClelland & Stewart

Atwood, Margaret, (1972), *Survival: A Thematic Guide to Canadian Literature*. Toronto: Anansi

Atwood, Margaret, (1985), *The Handmaid's Tale*. Toronto: Fawcett Crest

Atwood, Margaret, (1988), *Cat's Eye*. Toronto: McClelland & Stewart

Atwood, Margaret, (2000), *The Blind Assassin*. Toronto: McClelland & Stewart

Atwood Margaret, (2003), *Oryx and Crake*. New York: Nan A. Talese

Brooks, Jeremy, Review, *The Sunday Times,* 27 May 1973

Lessing, Doris, (1962), *The Golden Notebook*. London: Michael Joseph

CHAPTER 2: OVERVIEW OF THEMES

Atwood, Margaret, (1996), *Alias Grace*. Toronto: McClelland & Stewart

Atwood, Margaret, (2003), *Oryx and Crake*. New York: Nan A. Talese

Atwood – in promotional material by Houghton Mifflin taken for the CBC interview, 1986, Box 149:4, Margaret Atwood Collection, Thomas Fisher Rare Book Library

Barr, Marleen S. (1987), *Alien to Femininity: Speculative Fiction and Feminist Theory*. New York: Greenwood Press

Broner, E. M. (1978), *A Weave of Women*. New York: Holt, Rinehart and Winston

Burgess, Anthony, (1962), *A Clockwork Orange*. London: Heinemann

Foucault, Michel, (1978), *The History of Sexuality. Vol. 1*. Toronto: Random House

Huxley, Aldous, (1932), *Brave New World*. London: Chatto & Windus

Kumar, Krishnan (1987), *Utopia and Anti-utopia in Modern Times*. Oxford: Blackwell

Lyotard, Jean-Francois, (1986), 'Defining the Postmodern' in During, S. (ed.) (1993) *The Cultural Studies Reader*. London: Routledge, pp. 142–5

Mather, Cotton, *The Writings of:* (http://www9.georgetown.edu/faculty/bassr/heath/syllabuild/iguide/mather.html) (accessed 17 December 2009)

Miller, Arthur, (1953), *The Crucible*. New York: Viking Press

Orwell, George, (1949), *Nineteen Eighty-four*. New York: Harcourt, Brace

Swift, Jonathan, (1729/1995), *A Modest Proposal*. London: Prometheus Books

Tolan, Fiona, (2007), *Margaret Atwood: Feminism and Fiction*. New York: Rodopi

CHAPTER 3: READING *THE HANDMAID'S TALE*

Atwood, Margaret, (1972), *Surfacing*. Toronto: McClelland & Stewart

Atwood, Margaret, (1988), *Cat's Eye*. Toronto: McClelland & Stewart

Atwood, Margaret, (1993), *The Robber Bride*. New York: Nan A. Talese

Atwood, Margaret, (2003), *Oryx and Crake*. New York: Nan A. Talese

Atwood, Margaret, (2009), *The Year of the Flood*. Toronto: McClelland & Stewart

Butler, Judith, (1990), *Gender Trouble: Feminism and the Subversion of Identity*. New York: Routledge

Butler, Judith, (1993), *Bodies That Matter: On the Discursive Limits of 'Sex'*. New York: Routledge

Foucault, Michel, (1978), *The History of Sexuality. Vol. 1*. Toronto: Random House

Huxley, Aldous, (1932), *Brave New World*. London: Chatto & Windus.

Orwell, George, (1949), *Nineteen Eighty-four*. New York: Harcourt, Brace

Schlink, Bernhard, (1997), *The Reader*. New York: Random House

Swift, Jonathan, (1729), *A Modest Proposal*

CHAPTER 4: RECEPTION AND INFLUENCE

An Interview with Margaret Atwood on Her Novel The Handmaid's Tale http://www.randomhouse.comesouces/bookgroup/handmaid-stale_bgc.html#interview) (accessed 17 December 2009)

Adachi, Ken, (1985), 'Atwood's futuristic fiction'. *The Sunday Star,* 29 September, p. G11

Bradbury, Ray, (1953), *Fahrenheit 451.* New York: Ballantine

Brooks Bouson, Jane, (1993), *Brutal choreographies: Oppositional strategies and narrative design in the novels of Margaret Atwood.* Amherst, MA: University of Massachusetts Press

Cooper, Pamela, (1995), 'Sexual Surveillance & Medical Authority in Two Versions of *The Handmaid's Tale*', *Journal of Popular Culture* 28:4, Spring, p. 49

Coughlin, Ellen, (1980), 'Margaret Atwood', *Books and Arts* 1, 12, 7 March, pp. 5–6

Davidson, Cathy N. (1986), 'A feminist 1984: Margaret Atwood talks about her exciting new novel'. *Ms*, 14 February, p. 24

Foucault, Michel, (1978), *The History of Sexuality. Vol. 1.* Toronto: Random House

Frye, Northrop, (1957), *Anatomy of Criticism.* Princeton: Princeton University Press

Fullbrook, Kate, (1990), *Free women: Ethics and aesthetics in twentieth-century women's fiction.* Hemel Hempstead: Harvester Wheatsheaf

Howells, Coral Ann, (2000), 'Transgressing genre: A generic approach to Margaret Atwood's Novels: *The Handmaid's Tale* and *Dystopia'* in Nischik, R. M. (ed.) *Margaret Atwood: works and impact.* Rochester, Camden House

Kaler, Anne K. (1989), 'A sister, dipped in blood: Satiric inversion of the formation techniques of women religious' in Margaret Atwood's novel *The Handmaid's Tale. Christianity and Literature*, 38 (2), Winter, pp. 43–62

Klarer, Mario, (1995), 'Orality and literacy as gender-supporting structures in Margaret Atwood's *The Handmaid's Tale'. Mosaic (Winnipeg)*, 28, (4), December, 129–143

McCarthy, Mary, (1986), Review. *Book Review.* 9 February. Available online at http://partners.nytimes.com/books/00/03/26/specials/mccarthy-atwood.html (Accessed 3 January 2008)

Nicholson, Colin, (ed.) (1994), 'Versions of History: *The Handmaid's Tale* and Its Dedicatees', in *Margaret Atwood: Writing and Subjectivity.* Houndmills: Macmillan

Sage, Lorna, (1986), 'Projections from a messy present'. *Times Literary Supplement*, March 21, p. 307

Swift, Jonathan, (1729), *A Modest Proposal*

Wilson, Sharon Rose, (1993), *Margaret Atwood's Fairy Tale Sexual Politics.* Jackson: University Press of Mississippi

Workman, Nancy V. (1989), 'Sufi mysticism in Margaret Atwood's *The Handmaid's Tale'*, *Studies in Canadian Literature*, 14, 2 http://www.lib.unb.ca/Texts/SCL/bin/get.cgi?directory=vol14_2/&filename=Workman.htm (accessed 22 January 2010)

Updike, John, (1986), Review. *The New Yorker,* 12 May , pp. 118–25

SUGGESTIONS FOR FURTHER READING

Further works by Margaret Atwood

Atwood, Margaret, (1976), *Lady Oracle*. Toronto: McClelland & Stewart

Atwood, Margaret, (1991), *Wilderness Tips and Other Stories*. Toronto: McClelland & Stewart

Atwood, Margaret, (1992), *Good Bones*. Toronto: Coach House Press

Selected criticism and reviews

Davidson, Cathy and Davidson, Arnold E., (eds) (1981), *The Art of Margaret Atwood: Essays in Criticism*. Toronto: Anansi

Dvorak, Marta, (1986), 'Margaret Atwood's Humour' in Howells, Coral Ann (ed.) *The Cambridge Companion to Margaret Atwood*. Cambridge, Cambridge University Press

Feuer, L. (1997), 'The Calculus of Love and Nightmare: "The Handmaid's Tale" and the dystopian tradition'. *CRITIQUE: Studies in Contemporary Fiction*, 38, (2), Winter, 83–96

Frye, Northrop, (1973), 'Varieties of Literary Utopias', in Frank E. Manuel (ed.), *Utopias and Utopian Thought*. London: Souvenir Press

Howells, Coral Ann, (1996), *Margaret Atwood*. Hampshire: Palgrave Macmillan

Howells, Coral Ann, (ed.) (2006), *The Cambridge Companion to Margaret Atwood*. Cambridge: Cambridge University Press

Moylan, Tom, (2000), *Scraps of the Untainted Sky: Science Fiction, Utopia, Dystopia*. Boulder, Colorado: Westview Press

Nischik, Reingard M. (ed.) (2000), *Margaret Atwood: Works and Impact*. Rochester: Camden House

Wilson, Sharon Rose, (ed.) (2003), *Margaret Atwood's Textual Assassinations*. Columbus: Ohio State University Press

INDEX

abortion 86, 112
Afghanistan 48, 68, 69
Al Jazeera 68
angels 41, 45, 47, 48, 69, 70, 71,
    94, 95
Atwood, Margaret:
    The Animals in that Country 2
    The Blind Assassin 2, 6
    Cat's Eye 6
    The Circle Game 2
    The Edible Woman 2, 134
    Good Bones 135
    Lady Oracle 134
    Oryx and Crake 17, 23,
        95, 135
    The Robber Bride 135
    Surfacing 2, 5, 66, 134
    *Survival : A Thematic Guide to
        Canadian Literature* 2, 5
    Wilderness Tips 135
    The Year of the Flood 95, 135
Aunts 15, 16, 18, 33, 41, 45, 63,
    71, 78, 79
Austen, Jane, *Pride and
    Prejudice* 117
Australia 14
autobiography 8, 39
    semi-fictionalised 20

Barth, John 4
Bible 22, 49, 67, 71, 85, 124
biblical 13, 39, 96, 122, 133
Bilhah 13, 39, 71, 133
Birthmobile 49, 74, 78
Bloom, Harold 134
BlyssPluss Pills 18
Bradbury, Ray, *Fahrenheit
    451* 127

Brave New World, Aldous
    Huxley 22, 23, 25, 26, 68,
    121, 122, 129
Burgess, Anthony, *A Clockwork
    Orange* 26
burka 52, 118

'Can Lit' 5
Canada 2, 14, 65, 69, 76, 129, 130
Canadian 4, 39
Catholicism 24
ceremony 61, 84, 100
Chaucer, Geoffrey, *The
    Canterbury Tales* 118
Clinton, Hillary 4
colonies 40, 43
comedy 2
Commander 12, 13, 14, 15, 18,
    27, 29, 32, 33, 34, 35, 37, 38,
    40, 41, 43, 44, 45, 46, 47, 49,
    55, 58, 59, 61, 67, 68, 70, 71,
    72, 80, 81, 83, 84, 90, 91, 93,
    85, 96, 98, 99, 102, 103, 104,
    106, 107, 114, 115, 116, 117,
    119, 125, 127
Compucard 16, 87
Cotton Mather 28, 132
crime 2

dissident 68
domestic bliss 12
domestic horror 97
Dworkin, Andrea 34
dystopia 24, 25, 27, 30, 68, 121,
    123, 124, 129

Econowives 14, 88
erotic 70